WHEN THE DARK MOTHER CALLS

THE INITIATORY JOURNEY OF A
MAGDALENE MYSTIC

TRISTA HAGGERTY

Published by:

Dragon Hill Press
PO Box 506
Cherry Valley, NY 13320
www.DragonHillPress.com

Cover art by Julia Jeffery

Copyright © 2023 Trista Haggerty

ISBN: 979-8-218-29125-9

The author disclaims responsibility for adverse effects or consequences from the misapplication or injudicious use of the information contained in this book. Mention of resources and associations does not imply an endorsement.

Table of Contents

The Sword

Initiation by Fire

The Cauldron

Initiation by Water

The Sacred Marriage

Acknowledgements

To Matthew, Jessi, Javier and Ricardo who fill my heart every day and have been my greatest teachers.

To the mystics who have walked before me, Helena Shik, Clarissa Pinkola Estes, R.J. Stewart, Mara Freeman, Doloris Ashcroft Nowicki, Gareth Knight, and Dion Fortune to name just a few. Their work with the inner landscape and the Western Mystery School Tradition has guided me home to my roots.

Foreword

"This is my continual path of initiation. My actions, my moments of truth, my times of confronting fear and overcoming struggles set the next initiation into motion. Unlike our ancient ancestors who used to create initiatory experiences by burying the initiate underground or having them cross a narrow bridge lined with crocodiles on either side, I rely on my life's experiences to initiate me."

This statement from Trista sums up what it is to follow the prompts given to us by the Dark Mother in collaboration with our own soul's unique unfolding of our authentic nature. Through the multitude of deaths and rebirths woven into the very fabric of the Divine Intelligence of the natural world, we are brilliantly guided.

Trista's intimate sharing is a beautiful honoring of her relationship with her life, as her teacher and mentor, Helena, opened the door for her to rediscover her feminine essential nature. Her story is such an authentic depiction of walking the path of the Goddess and returning to a purity of heart, that you can feel it vibrate through your whole being.

She has clearly taken her well-deserved seat as a gatekeeper for others who are called by the Dark Mother, with a depth of empirical knowledge that is rare and sacred.

Mary Lane, author of *Divine Nourishment & Meena*

Introduction

*"Call it a dream or 'the treasure hard to attain';
call it a vocation or the awakening of one's innate genius.
Call it what you will, upon hearing the call we must follow
or else lose the true thread of our lives."*
— MICHAEL MEADE

At age 28, my life as I knew it, fell apart. I was a young mother and wife with a clear plan for my life that was rooted in a traditional, Christian upbringing in a small, rural town in Upstate New York. But one moment tossed all that I knew into chaos and started me on a journey to reclaim my roots as a mystic and priestess of the Magdalene traditions.

I traveled to many foreign countries visiting ancient sacred sites from some of the world's oldest religions. Many of these were magnificent, and remarkably intact such as the temples in Egypt. Others were half-buried stones, mere outlines of what once was, leaving much to the imagination.

I was unprepared for the effect these places would have on me. They altered my consciousness to such a degree, that when I returned home, my life no longer fit. That's when the real work began. My home life mirrored to me my own patterns and belief systems shaped by patriarchal thought and it was challenging to dismantle. Finding my voice, speaking my truth, trusting what was in my heart and aligning with the Divine became my daily practice. I didn't want to leave situations that weren't conducive to who I was becoming, but instead, learn how to influence change with love and grace, and not force.

It was not an easy path as I unearthed my forgotten self from a forgotten faith. I felt the pain of my own self-betrayal, the shame of victimhood and the agony of repression.

As much as I would have liked to have had a map during my years of pilgrimage, I didn't. I relied on my intuition, trusting each step I took. It wasn't until I wrote this book that the pieces started coming together, and I finally understood what I was doing all these years, and my ties to the ancient past.

I hope my story provides you with inspiration and a sense of sisterhood.

The Sword
Initiation by Fire

The sword is a Celtic symbol that relates to the element of fire for it is metal that has been shaped by the roaring fire of a forge. In life, we have challenges and events that stretch us beyond what we can ever imagine being able to handle and remain still intact. It is only by the strength of our will and personal integrity that we are able to persevere. These occurrences are life's initiations by fire. We reclaim our voices and stand up for our personal truths.

When we are voicing a truth for all of humanity, then the sword of truth is given to us by the Goddess. We are granted the magical powers and the undeniable strength to speak and do our bidding on Her behalf. But before this happens, we need to prove that we are strong enough and courageous enough to speak for all of humanity rather than be self-serving.

The sword also has the power of polarity. It cuts away that which no longer serves us.

Chapter 1
Truth Emerges

The blazing, hot sword of truth pierces my heart, shattering all illusions, cutting all threads that bind me to a life of lies. I am naked, stripped bare of my persona, surrendering to my truth that has been buried deep in the chamber of my own heart.

It's the little things that get you, every time. I wipe down the counter in our master bathroom and feel something just behind the mirror that rests on the tile. My fingers search the small space and pull out a gold, encased lipstick. It isn't mine. I freeze as my mind races in a million different directions. I cautiously open it. The bright red lipstick is like a neon sign, signaling to me danger. I feel neither rage nor sadness, but instead I'm paralyzed, not knowing how to respond or, to what I am responding to. Hand trembling, I carefully place the lipstick back behind the mirror. I'm not ready to face the answers to my questions. I walk into my bedroom where the kids are playing, so sweet and innocent. How is this moment going to change their lives? I want so badly to turn back the hands of time, just a few minutes, and undo what I found, but the enchantment of our safe little world is undeniably shattered. With a forced smile, I continue on with my day not knowing what else to do.

I say nothing to my husband until a few weeks later, when I find my lingerie stretched to proportions far greater than mine.

Suddenly, I understand his absence in both home and bed. I think back to an evening when we were getting ready to meet one of his clients for dinner. I had just put on a black, sleeveless dress that was open in the back all the way down to my waist. As I was slipping on my high heels, I noticed my husband looking at me. It wasn't a look of lust or desire or love. It was the look of jealousy. I'm both distraught and relieved. An odd and confusing feeling. Something I hadn't understood, now makes complete sense.

"Dan, we need to talk about this," I plead one evening after putting the kids to bed.

"I don't need to talk about it," he responds calmly, through clenched teeth.

It's a secret he'll take to his grave.

His hidden desire to be a woman turns to shame and spills out on the kids and me as anger and control, a temper that feels like a ticking time bomb. His refusal to get marriage counseling makes it impossible to find resolution, and his simmering anger scares me. I slip into a very dark place as I watch my life fall apart.

All I've ever dreamed of is being a mother and having a happy family. But now, that's all crumbling. I read that your first love is more about your fantasy of what love is. I realize that I've been living a dream, buying into what I wanted to believe our marriage was, while ignoring signs that speak of a different reality.

My strong, motherly instincts are the only thing that keep me from drowning in a bottomless sea of darkness and despair. I continue with my daily tending to both the home and the children, but on the inside, I feel dead, drained of all hope.

Jessi, who has just started walking, holds my hand and yanks really hard as if trying to snap me out of my faraway thoughts.

Sorry sweetie. Believe me, I don't want to be in this place. I don't know what's going on. Don't give up on me. Keep yanking.

I trudge through my days as I descend into darkness, a spiritual death that leaves me questioning the meaning of my life, offering only a single lifeline — faith. Faith that somehow, I'll be saved.

And I am saved. I turn on the TV, and Phil Donahue and his talk show guest, a woman who communicates with angels, opens the doors to my redemption. A middle-aged woman speaks with such strong convictions about her conversations with angels. Her words trigger a long forgotten memory and an immediate awakening. The doors fly open and just like that, my year spent in darkness drops away, and I stand on the threshold to a new life filled with hope and wonder.

I have a new-found interest. I start studying spiritual texts and reading books on energy healing, drinking in whatever information I can find, nourishing my parched soul. I try sharing this with my husband, but it makes him even more angry. I'm tormented daily by a ping pong match going on inside my head. *Should I go? Should I stay?* I cling to threads of hope that I can save my marriage, but in the end, realize that I am the only one trying to save it.

The weather forecasts a blizzard later in the day. Dan stays home and works out of his office. His presence matches the clouds, ominous and heavy. He's grown more and more distant and harder to be around.

"C'mon kids, let's get ready to go outdoors," I say, as they finish eating their breakfast muffins. Going outdoors is a welcome reprieve. It's something we do every day, but especially when Dan is home. He likes the house quiet so he can work.

After getting snow pants on, tying up boots, finding hats and mittens that match, and zipping up coats, the three of us trudge outdoors with Bradford, our golden retriever, leading the way.

We head into the woods behind our house, and I spot some deer tracks.

Matthew follows the tracks while Jessi is content grabbing onto the low-hanging hemlock branches and watching the snow fall off. This is where I find my peace, in the woods, exploring with the kids.

Before heading back inside, we lay down on the snow-covered ground and make snow angels. The kids giggle as snowflakes land on their faces. I know this is one of those moments I'll always treasure. A simple, undefined moment of just being together, experiencing the beauty of nature. A feeling of contentment washes over me, something I haven't felt in a while. As I lie in the soft snow, the sound of birds chirping and the kids giggling becomes hushed. A thought, a feeling, or maybe a message—I'm not quite sure, but I know there's someone I need to find. Someone that is important to me. A person who is going to help me learn more about the healing work I'm studying. I explore the feeling more, but suddenly, Bradford reappears and jumps on the three of us, grabbing our hats.

The feeling there is someone I need to find persists for weeks. After calling a few healing centers and massage therapists, I'm given a name and phone number of a woman that lives a few towns over at the top of Putney Mountain. I call her and schedule a session. We talk only briefly, but hearing her voice for the first time, feels like home.

Two weeks later, I grip the steering wheel of my Jeep like my life depends on it, barreling through the torrents of rain and fog, at times spinning my wheels. It's a dark, rainy, March night in Vermont. The road is narrow and bumpy with tire tracks and deep grooves filled with muddy slush. I stop momentarily to check the directions scribbled on a small piece of scrap paper. Not sure if I missed a turn, I hesitantly continue. There are no houses to light the way, only the soft glow of the moon reflecting off the snow covered woods.

My heart beats fast, like a drum pounding in my chest. *What if I'm lost? What if I'm too late and she refuses to see me?* I've waited two weeks for this session, and the thought of missing it and having to wait longer is unsettling.

Slowing down to check my directions, through the fog, I see lights up ahead. I go a little further and turn into a driveway. The small, rustic Cape Cod style home is a welcome sight and matches the description she'd given to me.

The soft glow from the windows is inviting. Pulling the hood of my raincoat over my head, I follow the stone footpath leading to her back door. I notice firewood neatly stacked along the walkway and the empty terra-cotta flowerpots stored nearby. Taking a deep breath, I knock on the old wooden door that quickly opens before I even finish knocking.

"Come in, come in!" she says. "You must be Treeeesta."

Here's the woman I've been looking for. Her warm welcome and unpretentious demeanor confirms this. She's nothing like a therapist sitting behind a desk in a sterile office with diplomas displayed on the walls. Helena is a petite, older German woman with long brown hair, pulled up and pinned loosely to the top of her head. She wears an oversized, gray sweater that looks cozy with purple leggings and big, wool socks. *I already love her.*

She leads me through her disheveled kitchen. Small bottles with rooting plants and dried seeds line her windowsills. Bundles of dried plants hang from the low ceiling. Candles burn, emitting a soft glow. Large crystals sit on the kitchen counter and other random spots throughout her house. Female statues, some engraved with strange symbols and others she's adorned with bright silk fabrics, sit prominently in small alcoves or on the center of an altar. All of this is foreign to me, other than the empty flower pots I spotted on my way in, and the wood pile. I have those, too. But that's it, just the pots and the wood pile are the only things about her home that are familiar. But that's okay. I'm ready for different. Anything that is other than what's expected.

My home, with its colonial decor, shows nothing of who I am. A safe facade. As strange as the crystals and statues are to me, deep inside my heart, I feel something stir.

Her home is like a cozy Hobbit house. Oriental rugs are scattered about the old wooden floors, worn from years of use. A large table covered with a bright blue and yellow flowered tablecloth sits at the end of her kitchen in front of two French doors leading to an outdoor deck.

I follow her into her dimly lit living room and climb onto her healing table that's sandwiched in-between an overstuffed couch and chair. I notice framed photos of children with a much younger version of herself, hanging on the walls.

"So, what brings you here on this stormy night?" she asks as she begins working on my feet.

"Well...I'm not really sure. I had a feeling I needed to find someone, and my search led me to you," I say, not sure where to begin.

I carefully study her as she looks off into the distance, like she's watching an invisible movie. She has dark brown eyes that are soft and twinkling one moment, and intense and fierce another.

"Aaaah," she says. "You're leaving your husband."

"No, no I'm not," I say with an unexpected defiance. "We're having some problems, but I have no plans on leaving."

"Hmmmm, that's not what I see," she says casually, completely untethered as to whether I agree or not and continues onto other subjects.

An hour passes by quickly, and before I know it, our time has come to an end. I carefully stand-up, feeling a bit dizzy. She had spent most of the time doing energy work on me, and I had slipped into a deep state of relaxation, sometimes falling asleep.

We spend a few moments sitting at her kitchen table. She explains to me briefly, about the work she does and gives me a brochure of her sacred journeys. I have a hard time leaving. I stand on a threshold to a new life that I have yet to understand, but know it has something to do with her.

I give her a hug goodbye and as I'm walking out the door, Helena says, "Treeesta, your children are going to be just fine." I nod my head. She knows what weighs heavy on my heart.

I lean up against the old pine tree where I watch the kids play in their sandbox. Tears erupt and carry the truth to the surface. I can no longer deny the disintegration of my marriage. I know it's over. My heart is empty where hope had once resided. Helena had been right. It took me over a year to come to terms with the truth.

I turn towards the cool, spring breeze, attempting to dry and soothe my swollen eyes. I'm going to miss the woods behind our house where the kids and I play and especially the old pine. I had leaned against the sturdy pine tree for the past year, voicing my inner battle as I faced the decision of whether or not I should leave my marriage. I'm not going to miss our big, fancy house, but instead the lilac bush where our bird feeder hangs and the maple tree that shades the kids while they play. As I get up to join the kids, I feel the energy of the pine tree wrap around me like a warm hug. More tears escape as I realize the tree has been listening all this time. I've always reached out to nature in times of despair, but this was the first time I felt nature reach back.

I sit on the edge of the sandbox peering into my children's eyes. I am busting apart their safe world, dismantling their childhood. I am doing that. Me alone. Their father would live this lie forever, but

I just can't. I can't go through the motions of fake happiness. I want my children to know me, not a false person living a lie.

As if hearing my thoughts, Matthew looks up at me with his big, bright blue eyes. Stares at me for a brief moment, saying nothing. I feel so exposed like getting caught doing something wrong. But I know my decision has been made. He then gives me the sweetest smile as if to say, "It's okay, we'll get through this."

Finally, one day, I'm able to muster up the courage and say to Dan, "I'm leaving. I'm taking the kids, and we're moving back to New York to be near family."

"Well, that's too bad. What if I put in a pool and a tennis court?" he says in a monotone voice. There is no sorrow nor pleading, just a business deal, at which he is highly skilled.

I empty my big walk-in closet, tearing silk dresses and sequin gowns from their hangers and throw them into boxes. I toss in my Louis Vuitton purse and countless pairs of high-heeled shoes. Every piece of clothing feels like a lie. By the time I get through, my closet contains very little — a few hand-knit sweaters and a stack of faded Levi jeans. I drop all the boxes off at the nearest Salvation Army.

Months later, with my Jeep filled with boxes, suitcases and toys, the kids squished into the backseat, and Bradford, in the front with me, we move back to my hometown, where my parents live, to begin a new life.

Chapter 2
The Mountains of Peru

The star beings call, "Come child, come. Come back to where you began and remember who you are." I answer, not knowing to what, but feel myself pulled by the luminous umbilical cord of mother earth. "Trust, trust," I hear the soft whispers. "It's okay to let go." So, I surrender to the swift current that carries me to lands faraway.

The rickety train winds its way through the Sacred Valley. I feel small and insignificant in comparison to the majestic height of the Andes Mountains. Their snow-capped rugged peaks sit atop the graceful folds of fading greenery that descend into the valley. It's June and winter in Peru. The sides of the mountains are dotted with small, earthen homes and terraced land for farming. Occasionally, the train passes a group of mountain people holding necklaces and colorful sweaters in their arms. They stand near the rail hoping the train will stop so they can sell their home-made wares to the passengers. They wear layers of clothes, woven in bright colors to combat the cold, and wide-brimmed, black hats that shade their sun-worn faces. The women wear their dark hair in long braids, framing their perfectly, round faces, some with toothless smiles that stretch from ear to ear. As the train slows to a stop, I see a woman running down the hill carrying a basket of hand-knit dolls, two small children running after her. The little girl carries a basket, too, and the boy holds onto a rope with a llama in tow.

My heart aches. It's been only a week since I joined Helena and the rest of the group, but it's the first time I've ever been away from Matthew and Jessi. Matthew is five and Jessi is only three. They're staying with my parents for the two weeks while I'm away. I miss them terribly. Part of me even feels angry that my life is pulling me in a direction that I don't understand, nor did I plan for.

Just a few months ago, I pulled the dog-eared brochure out of the drawer of my night stand. I re-read it, and with reservation, gave Helena a call. I intuitively knew the call was going to lead me to signing up for one of her trips, but I couldn't yet admit it to myself. I wasn't ready to leave my children. The demands felt too great, but the calling that stirred deep in my belly was difficult to ignore. My internal compass pulled me in one direction as I resisted and clung to the few familiar threads remaining in my life, but eventually all gave way. My mother would have never ventured off, away from the family to explore and ponder her life. I'm in a foreign landscape in more ways than one.

I open up the small window next to my seat and lean out, waving to the woman with the basket of dolls. She hurries over as I stretch my arm towards her, holding money in one hand while pointing with the other. She takes my money in exchange for two dolls, nods her head in appreciation and moves onto the next eager tourist. The hand-knit dolls wear traditional Peruvian clothes. I smile and sit them on my lap, occupying the space where my children aren't.

Now, here I am, riding on a train with a small group of people I've just met, through a foreign landscape, putting my life back together in a way that is real and authentic, where there are no lies and hidden secrets.

Peru holds all the beauty and magic I need to remedy my despair and inspire me to create a new life. While the cities lack adequate housing, according to our standards of living in the United States, the people seem happy and content. The peasants, as they are re-ferred to by their own people, live out in the countryside, up in the hills. They have small, mud huts for homes, gardens where they grow much of their own food and a goat or a llama that serve as their pack animal and travel with them wherever they go. I think the peasants have the richest of lives living in wide open spaces, growing their own food, and making their own bread with the grains they grow. Their simple way of living is appealing.

We arrive in Aguas Calientes, a small town at the base below Machu Picchu. Here, we board an old bus that smells of exhaust fumes and rumbles loudly as it winds its way up an incredibly narrow road leading to the ruins. Looking out the window, I can't see the edge of the road, only the sheer drop-off below. I close my eyes, praying we won't topple over the side of the mountain.

Finally, we arrive safely at the masterpiece, Machu Picchu, the ancient Inca citadel tucked away, high up in the Andes. Our hotel, a small, simple lodge, is the only lodging within the bounds of the ruins. Helena hands out room keys, and we all scatter to our rooms with bags in hand. I have just enough time to explore the ruins before meeting everyone for dinner.

I quickly drop my bags off in my room and go to explore. Being "off season" in Peru, I'm the only one walking around other than a couple of our group members.

I follow a narrow footpath that leads to a complex of stone structures — houses, temples and sanctuaries, all built with large field stones, amazingly still intact. Resting on one of the stone walls, I gaze out to the mountains and the breathtaking view. A vast wilderness surrounds Machu Picchu. I remember Helena saying that the Incas worshipped the sun as their deity, and I understand why they built their city here. I feel closer to the sun and sky, and to God. Directly below me is a vestige of countless, small farming plateaus that scale up the side of the mountain. Each plateau is connected by thousands of stone steps where crops once grew, but now only grass.

The power of Machu Picchu is undeniable and more than I can handle. I feel unhinged with no sure foundation, completely ungrounded, almost shaky, like at any moment I'll be swept up into the sky. There's an increasing high pitched buzzing noise in my head, and I cover my ears with my hands, even though I know it isn't coming from outside of me. Intuitively, I slip off my sandals to feel the ground beneath my feet and turn to see a llama walking towards me. It stops and stands about 7 feet away, its jaw moving back and forth as it casually chews, staring at me with its big brown eyes and long lashes. I smile and try to coax it closer, but it's content on keeping a safe distance. I imagine the llama being a guide sent to calm my nerves. The buzzing sound stops, and I feel more grounded. Thanking the llama for her presence, I continue following more narrow footpaths as I wander through the ancient city.

That evening, our group meets in the hotel's restaurant for dinner where we sample traditional Peruvian foods, like Antichuchos, marinated, grilled beef hearts and Cuy Chactado, baked guinea pig. The foods are flavored with spices that leave my mouth tingling — yet another new experience. I feel small at times, being the youngest of the group and the least worldly. I had never traveled to a foreign country before this trip. I listen intently to William share his experience from the year prior when he had a sudden heart attack. His eloquent storytelling combined with his English accent makes the most frightening experience of his life sound like a fairy tale. And Jocelyn, she's fascinating to watch. She's the epitome of an older English woman until she interacts with our waiter. She then speaks fluent Spanish and abandons all properness. She becomes sexy and flirty as her Spanish words roll across her tongue. Her hands, once still and controlled, are now animated. There are several other women from the States, well-traveled and all much older than me. Often during our meals, I sit back and listen to their countless stories of far off places, questioning whether I dare to dream of living such a life and feeling I have little to contribute to the conversations.

The next morning, I wake at sunrise and peek out the small window of my hotel room. The sun slowly rises above one of the mountain peaks that surround Machu Picchu, creating an emerald-green glow. I'm rooming with a woman named Jill who is a little older than me and a real free spirit. She spent the past 10 years traveling and working as a chef at high-end hotels. Such a contrast to my life as a mom. She's so down to earth, and I really enjoy getting to know her.

Jill and I, barely awake, pull on our jeans, t-shirts, hiking boots and grab our backpacks. We meet the rest of the group in the lobby where we buy water, or agua, for the day. We're preparing to climb Wayna (Huayna) Picchu, the "Mountain of Death", a tall mountain that sits directly across from Machu Picchu. It's an all-day hike, up and down, so we want to get an early start.

Helena leads us through dense foliage on a walkway paved with black top.

"This is a pretty easy hike!" I say to Jill.

"Yeah, it's such a gentle incline, not bad at all," she responds.

But to our group's surprise, past the dense foliage, the trail goes from being pleasant to treacherous with a steep incline. At this point, our group spreads out, each person focused on the challenging climb ahead.

Our paved walkway turns into a narrow, well-worn, dirt footpath and at times, steep, stone steps with no railing or ropes to hold onto. Trees and roots that jut out from the sides of the mountain are my lifelines as I frequently use them to pull me up the trail. The climb takes every ounce of my focus and determination.

Since each group member is climbing at their own pace, I'm left to my own thoughts and inner experience. As I'm about halfway up, I meet a small, wiry and much older woman who's on her way down.

"You definitely don't want to go all the way up to the top," she says as she passes me, her tone gruff. "It's super scary and dangerous."

"Okay, thanks for the heads up," I respond as I wave her cigarette smoke away from my face.

I continue on with my hike, not fully aware as to how much the woman's message has influenced me. Eventually, I reach the high plateau where many hikers are resting, enjoying the view. I sit for a while and take my boots off. My feet are hot and my legs tired. I pull my water bottle and granola bar out of my backpack and spend about a half hour resting. The view is amazing. Beautiful, lush green foliage drapes the sides of the Andes Mountains that surround us in all directions. I feel really proud of myself. I'm so far from home in many ways. Physically very far, and very far out of my comfort zone too. I haven't really ever done anything adventurous other than leave home to attend college in Boston at age 18.

I now understand what the woman meant by going to the very top. While the plateau can be considered the top, it isn't. To get to the very peak means crawling on my hands and knees through a rocky overhang on the side of the mountain. I decide I'm close enough to the top and get ready to head back down.

Putting my boots back on, I begin my descent down the mountain which is just as treacherous as the climb up. But I struggle with the fact that I haven't gone all the way to the top. As I near the halfway point down the mountain, I can no longer ignore my inner voice nagging me, so I stop to listen.

Why did I let that woman's comment influence me?

It's a crushing realization of seeing the many times in my life where I've let others' opinions alter my decisions. I've let fear dictate too much of my life. I wonder what my life would have looked like if I had never let fear make my decisions for me.

Damn it! I have to go up to the top!

I want to scream, but instead, turn around and start climbing with sheer determination to make it all the way to the top, conquering both the mountain and my fears.

I know what your whispers sound like, fear, and I'm not going to listen to you any longer.

With each step, memories of things I've wanted to do but didn't because I was too afraid, play in my mind like an ongoing slide show. I wanted to be an actress when I was little but was too afraid to get up on a stage in front of people. I wanted to go to college to be an interior decorator, but my mom and dad told me I'd never find a job. When I was nine, I wanted so badly to learn how to ride a horse. I was intimidated by their power and size but loved them. That changed quickly with my first lesson. It wasn't the horse I was afraid of, it was the teacher. He was big and tall with a booming voice and instructed the young riders like a military sergeant.

Did I marry my husband out of fear, too?

All the times I'd made decisions based on fear and chose the safe and acceptable road led me further away from myself. I grieve the loss of what might have been. Such a different landscape stretched out before me in my mind of how my life could have been different. I'm determined to never let this happen again.

I've given too much credit to fate and destiny as though I've had no choice. When things haven't worked out in my life, it's been comforting to believe it was because of something out of my control. I'm waking up to the reality that I'm the sole creator of my life. A painful realization, but at the same time, liberating.

My legs are already tired, and my hands blistered, but my drive and determination to undo all the fear I've let influence me over the years is what gets me to the top.

On my way up, I meet another woman coming down. We both step aside to let each other pass. She is glowing, with a huge smile and bright eyes. Such a contrast to the first woman I encountered.

"You're going to absolutely love climbing to the very top!" she says with a big smile. "It's just so extraordinary!"

I smile and thank her. Her beautiful presence tells me I'm on the right path. A life-defining moment where I put a sticky note in my soul's memory bank, "Don't let fear dictate your life. It will lead to struggle."

I make it back up to the plateau. There are no members of our group there, and I know I'm completely on my own. I continue on the footpath that leads me to the rocky overhang. Abandoning my backpack, I lay down on my stomach, and pull myself with my arms through the narrow, dirt passage. I feel like I'm coming out of a birth canal, being born into a new life. Beyond the overhang, the narrow footpath continues, edged with short tufts of grass as the only barrier to the sheer drop-off. Clinging to the rocky face of the mountain on my left, I carefully place each foot, one in front of the other until I reach the very top of Wayna Picchu.

The top is small and grassy, about six or seven feet in diameter with jagged rocks jutting out over the edge. It's scary, but awesome and magnificent. I climb onto one of the larger rocks that appear to hang in mid-air over the side of the mountain, anchored only at one end. I sit as long as my nerves allow, which isn't very long.

It's terrifying. I'm relieved to slide down off the stone and back onto the small patch of grass. As my breath returns to normal and I relax, I thank both women who were so purposefully placed on my path to teach me about fear and how to follow my heart.

Feeling inspired, I head back down the mountain, careful with each step and taking my time. I meet up with Jill on the very last leg of the trail. Both of us are so physically exhausted, our legs are shaking. We fall to the ground laughing at ourselves, and crawl on our hands and knees up the last few steps of Machu Picchu to our hotel.

After a hot shower that soothes my sore muscles, I meet our group downstairs for dinner. The usual chatter and laughing is now hushed as everyone quietly enjoys their meal, too tired to talk. Helena announces she wants to meet at 2:00 in the morning out in the ruins. No one says anything, but their eyes clearly say, "Are you kidding me?"

"It's much easier to listen to what the stones have to say without the distraction of other people around," she explains to our tired group. "There's also something magical about that time of night. You can more easily slip into other worlds," she continues.

Most of the members of our group bow out of Helena's plan, but I want to experience what it's like. I don't know what she means by "other worlds", but there's a lot that Helena says that I don't understand. She frequently mentions portals and encoded land. I never question it because it's a language that intuitively feels right and oddly familiar.

And so, at two in the morning, I wake Jill. We throw on our clothes and stumble down to the lobby, still half asleep, to meet Helena.

Helena leads Jill and me out to the top of Machu Picchu. The air is cool, and it jolts me awake. I look at the sky, an endless sea of blackness dotted with bright twinkling stars. Not a single sound breaks the silence. No traffic, no city lights in the distance, an impeccable stillness, a gentle and embracing power.

Helena calls in the gods and goddesses of Peru and then honors the four directions. All else drops away into stillness. She comes over and stands behind both Jill and me, presenting us for initiation. Chills run up and down my spine coupled with awe. I'm standing at the top of Machu Picchu getting initiated into the sky mysteries. Even though I don't know what the sky mysteries are, I don't care, it's exciting. I've never done anything like this before.

Helena quietly guides both of us over to a cluster of very large stones and instructs us to lean into them, close our eyes and meditate. We lean on the stones, face forward, pressing our bellies to the cold, rough surface. I let the warmth of my body warm the stone, wrapping my arms around it, still feeling so tired.

Am I doing this right? What am I supposed to be feeling? I love Helena's cape. She looks like a wizard, or more like a witch. I'm sure she gets that a lot. Stop thinking!

Finally, exasperated, I convince myself that none of it matters anyway.

Just be here, be present, let go. And for God's sake, shut up!

My mind stops its incessant chatter, and I sink deeper into myself. The boundary between my body and the surface of the rock melts away. I almost gasp, but know I'll lose the sensation if I do, so remain calm. I merge with the rock, feeling its weight and incredible depth of being and oddly, it feels very fluid. I sense being inside the stone, like an old chamber or an old stone library that holds knowledge. There are no words that come to me, instead it's a feeling of ancient wisdom that predates language. Maybe the language of symbols, yet no images come to me. It's beyond what I can comprehend. The flexibility of my body is gone and instead, I feel as I imagine a rock would. Heavy, solid, stationary, and ancient. I sense the rock has a very specific purpose and is a part of a very large network of other rocks that act as anchors like pieces to a large puzzle.

I could stay in this space for hours communing with the rock, but an owl hoots in the distance, and the sound pulls me back to my body. I give Helena a wide-eyed, mouth-hanging-open look. She just smiles and winks. Her all-knowing eyes bring me much comfort.

Jill and I quietly follow Helena up the ancient stone steps to the highest plateau, often called the Sacred Plaza. The moonlight is bright enough to illuminate the Intihauntana stone that stands in the center of the plaza, a large stone believed to be used for astronomical purposes.

Helena shares with us that many of the altar stones that people believe to be for astronomical purposes are more than just sun dials. And this, I feel, is the case with Machu Picchu's Intihauntana stone. It marks the exact moment of the spring and fall equinoxes and is nicknamed, *The Hitching Post of the Sun*. The Incas believed the stone held the powers of the sun — the power to illuminate what lays hidden.

Jill and I take turns lying on the stone next to the pillar that protrudes out of the center as Helena stands watch. The stone is cool, as is the night air. I lay facing up to the starlit sky and close my eyes, resting, still so tired from my earlier climb. And then I'm out. I don't remember anything. It's like suddenly being knocked unconscious. Moments later, I jolt awake with a gasp. *Had I fallen asleep?* Helena reaches for my arm to help me off the stone.

"I thought we were going to lose you to the stars," she says, looking at me intently.

"What just happened?" I ask Helena. I'm confused and disoriented like when you're suddenly woken in the middle of the night, one foot in this world and one foot in the dreamworld.

"It's the stone," Helena says matter of factly. "It opens the doorway to your destiny and brings past-life memories to the present," she says, with her head tilted and arms crossed, studying me.

"You're good, sweetie! Now let's get back to the hotel and get some sleep," she says clapping her hands together as if having just completed her task.

The three of us walk back to the hotel arm in arm. I have questions, but I'm barely able to keep my eyes open, much less talk coherently. I just want to curl up in bed and sleep.

Our few remaining days speed by and soon our trip comes to an end. We gather for our farewell dinner, an elaborate buffet of ceviche, cold fish and marinated beef, and Papas a la Huancaina— potatoes in a creamy, cheese sauce served with a pit-roasted, guinea pig. There's a group of men playing pan pipes as we eat, drink wine and dance. It's the perfect ending to a magical journey.

This trip has been such an important beginning. I was able to penetrate the foundation of fear that I had been so fully anchored in. I imagined myself like a tree growing on top of cement, a man-made foundation with very little fertile soil to grow, completely dependent on mankind. An impenetrable foundation that inhibits growth in every way. But now, having freed myself from fear, my roots sink deep into the dark fertile soil of the mother, nourished by truth and her life-giving source. The perfect place to begin to build a new life.

Chapter 3

Dismantling Fear

Truth stalks me. It's penetrated the veil of illusion known as FEAR and reveals itself at every turn. I now walk with a foot in both worlds — one in the manmade and one in truth. And trust me, they are very different worlds.

Driving down the tree-lined road from our house to my children's school, I notice a group of men in a field dismantling an old, dilapidated barn. *Someone's finally taking that thing down.* For years, the barn, with its weathered boards, sat in the field, leaning feebly to the right, looking as though it was going to collapse with the slightest gust of wind.

The dismantling progresses throughout the week until, eventually, there is nothing left. I have mixed feelings. The barn has been part of the landscape for as long as I can remember, and I feel a pang of sadness as if saying goodbye to an old friend. The area is cleared of every last bit of weathered wood, leaving an open, airy space that feels naked as I can now see into the forest, once blocked from view. The following week, as I drive by, I notice a work crew and a stack of brand, new lumber. I am excited to see what they were building.

I watch this scene play out every day as I drive by. I can't help but relate it to my own experience. A couple months has passed since my trip to Peru. Returning home feels like a visit to another foreign landscape. Becoming so aware of my fears during that trip also makes me aware of the fear in our culture. I'm going through my own dismantling, tearing down my weathered beliefs that no longer serve me. I desperately want to clear a space so I can build my new life in a way that's aligned with my emerging self.

As I walk Matthew to his first day of kindergarten, I hold back tears and manage a false smile. Walking through the main entrance, my nose wrinkles and my stomach turns at the smell of industrial cleaning products hanging in the air. *Matthew's going to have to breathe this in all day.*

Memories surface of trying to fit in at my school as a child, the expectations, and a few unkind teachers. And now, here I am, walking my own son into the same school I had attended. It feels like a death sentence. Of his innocence. Of his wonder. Of his growing imagination and curiosity. This place will kill his experience of life as a magical place. I don't want to let go of his hand holding so tightly to mine. "Let's forget about all this and run away!" I want to say, but I know that isn't a viable solution.

We walk down the long hallway and find his classroom. His little hand slips from mine as he crosses the threshold into the world, for now, encapsulated in a small classroom with bright-colored Legos and giant letters of the alphabet displayed on posters throughout the room.

I bend down and give him a quick hug. "You have a great first day," I say, my voice shaking as I hold back tears. I watch him tentatively join a group of other kids, followed by one last look over his shoulder to see if I'm still here. I give a little wave and duck out of the room. I can't get out fast enough before tears escape.

Up until this point, I had spent all my life trying to fit into this man-made world. I was a daughter of the patriarch, my father's daughter. I had worked hard to get good grades and become the person that both my parents and society expected of me. I graduated from college, had a short-lived career, and married a successful businessman. Striving to meet my goals was fueled by an underlying fear that something horrible was going to happen if I failed a class, didn't succeed, or veered from the path of normalcy. It's like walking through life with my breath held, inhaling just enough air, but never truly sinking into my own being.

But now, here I am. I'm seeking power, not in the world of the patriarch, but inside myself.

As a young girl, I turned to the role-model that held the power in the family and that was my father. He had the final word on everything. I'm sure my mother heavily influenced my dad's decisions in her own quiet way, but on a day to day basis, it appeared to be my dad who held all the power. I turned away from my mother, seeing her and the nature of the feminine as having no power. And, as a result, betrayed myself until the Dark Mother came calling and invited me into my inner landscape, to my roots. Exhausted and overwhelmed from trying to maintain my false life, I crawled to her feet as I realized what I'd done. Here, in the depths of my own womb-like cave, I lick my wounds and begin the arduous journey to reclaim my power. A power with few role models, only some vague memories from the past — a temple priestess, a medicine woman, a witch — memories that become more relevant and palpable as my soul is stirred awake.

Since Jessi started pre-school the same week, I return home to a deafeningly quiet house.

Later that week, I have a dream.

I'm walking along a stone pathway. I look at my feet and see a pair of old leather straps for sandals and the hem of my dark, wool cape. I'm heading to a stone building that feels like a sanctuary or a temple. I'm carrying a basket filled with roots and other plants. I open the door and several young girls greet me with big smiles, eager to see what I'm carrying in my basket. There are other women there. One working at a loom, another grinding something in a large wooden bowl with a stone she holds in her hand. As I turn to shut the door, I notice a large field with several tall stones standing on end. There's a path to the right leading down to the cliffs near the sea.

The kids are still sound asleep next to me when I wake early the following morning. I lay very still, as I work hard to recall my dream, afraid any movement will send it reeling to the far end of my memory. I don't want to leave this dreamscape that feels so nourishing, like home.

I have a foot in both worlds. One foot in the here and now. And the other foot in what appears to be an ancient Goddess culture where children were taught to trust their intuition and the magic of life, particularly in nature. I have a vague memory of children being taught about the power of their imagination as the first step to creating their reality. Nature has a mythic quality to it, providing an emotional connection. A tree wasn't just a tree, it was a friend, like the old grandfather oak.

These memories and deep truths come to me as whispers screaming to my heart. I'm painfully aware what I had turned away from all these years. Myself, my true nature, abandoned in the wild as I signed over my soul in a contract with society to become like everyone else. I believed it all important, necessary to succeed in this world like stepping onto a conveyor belt and becoming fac-tory-made — the perfect house, the perfect job, and the perfect husband. From the outside appearance, I had all that, but it was nothing, an empty shell, and a lie.

Now, I crave a hand-made life, imperfect, unique, wild, belonging to no one else but me.

I quietly climb out of bed and pull on my old worn jeans and hand knit sweater. With tail wagging, Bradford follows me down the stairs. I open the back door to let him out and stand on the threshold admiring the beauty. The chilly morning air smells fresh and sweet, and the sun's rays illuminate the vibrant fall colors of the maple trees behind our house. I remember myself as a little kid staring out of the classroom window with fingers pressed upon the glass, seeing freedom in the woods beyond, but unable to touch it. I step onto the frost covered grass, my bare feet tingling from the cold. I hear a black crow cawing from the top of the tree as if welcoming me back to the wild.

As I dismantle the world I grew up in, my connection to the ancient Goddess culture reveals itself. In my dreams, I see images of stone courtyards and women living together in simpler ways that flow with the seasons. Young women being taught to honor the ways of Mother Earth and the Goddess. They're encouraged to use their intuition and are respected for their unique gifts, a different kind of schooling. The memories play throughout my dreams like an ongoing movie, magnifying my grief over our current school system and way of life. I desperately want to return to that life yet have no idea how to create it in the modern-day world.

The more I remember, the more rage creeps in. I feel robbed of a way of life more congruent with my true self. Cheated of something that feels rightfully mine. The world has kept a secret from me, and I'm waking up and remembering.

I wonder if this is a shared sorrow among women — an ache in our hearts, a longing for sisterhood, a faint memory of living in community with one another. The suffering and the misery over what's been lost, and the grief of conceding to the only option presented gets buried deep in our wombs, almost forgotten.

My rage brews, but I keep it contained. I don't want it to spill out on the school, nor anyone else. Through clenched teeth, I continue going through the day to day motions in life finding respite in my continual dreams.

Fall quickly speeds by and before I know it, the trees are bare except for the stubborn leaves of the old oaks. Each day greets us with a thick frost that sparkles in the morning sun.

One evening, I sit squished between Matthew and Jessi in our small family bed. I read them a bed-time story and they start giggling. "What's so funny?" I ask them, smiling.

"Why do you sound like an Irish person when you're reading to us? It sounds weird."

I laugh. "I know, I don't know why. Every time I start reading, an Irish accent comes through."

True and so strange. Later that night, I wake from another dream similar to my others. Always a group of women, many wearing wool capes, a stone circle in the distance and a loom nearby. This time, I don't feel joy in the dream. I feel panic. In the dream, we hurry and dig in a dirt floor to hide. I wake up sweating, trying to dislodge myself from the scene.

The following morning, I drop Matthew off at school, drive Jessi to her preschool and then head to the library.

I find several books on stone circles, discovering that they were primarily built in the British Isles. Chills run up my spine as I turn the page — a full-color image of a stone circle exactly like the one in my dreams is spread across the page with a small caption that reads, "Ring of Kerry, Ireland." I hurriedly sign the book out and head home to call Helena.

"Hi Helena. It's Trista."

"Hiiiii! How are you Treeeesta?"

"I'm good. Just getting settled into our new home."

It's always so good to hear her voice. We chat for a while about the kids. Helena, being a mom and a new grandmother, always asks about Matthew and Jessi. She gets it. She holds the role of being a mother as a sacred duty, and I so appreciate her wisdom from her years of raising three children.

"So… there's a reason for my call besides just checking in. I've been having dreams all winter, and I had one just last night. It feels like a past life, and almost in every dream there's a stone circle in the distance. So today, I went to the library and looked up stone circles and I swear, I saw the same one that was in my dream. It was in Ireland."

Hearing the door to my kitchen open, I turn to see my friend Kelly coming in, carrying a basket of bread. Motioning to her to sit down, I return my attention to Helena.

"Oh! That's so interesting," Helena says. "I'm just putting together my itinerary for the new year, and I've added visiting Ireland as an addition to my trip to the British Isles."

"No! Really? That's awesome! When is it?" I ask. Timing is everything to me when it comes to these trips. I need months to save money, and I like to plan way ahead to make sure the kids are well prepared and taken care of while I'm gone.

"I don't have the exact dates yet, but it will be sometime in August."

"Perfect! That gives me plenty of time to prepare." Eight months.

"I feel like you're going to be bringing someone with you," says Helena. My eyes quickly dart to Kelly.

As Helena continues talking, I point at her and mouth the words, "You need to talk to her."

Kelly, shaking her head whispers, "No, why? I don't want to."

"Yes, you need to," I mouth back to her.

"Helena, I think I know who you're seeing coming to Ireland with me. It's my friend Kelly who just happens to be sitting right here. I'm going to pass the phone over." I hurriedly hand her the phone, unable to conceal my excitement.

Rolling her eyes and giving me an exasperated look, she reluctantly takes the phone.

Kelly and I had become fast friends since meeting a few months prior at our daughters' preschool. While Kelly is several years younger, I feel as though I've known her forever. She's a soul sister, and we share similar views on how to raise our children. Kelly's also a baker. She makes wedding cakes that are nothing short of a sculpted work of art. Each bite is pure joy served on a plate.

I watch Kelly nod her head as Helena continues talking. Her initial resistance drops away. She's listening intently, her eyes softening and her cheeks blush.

"Well…what do you think?" I ask her as she hangs up the phone.

"I…I guess I'm going." Kelly looks a bit stunned. During her brief conversation, Helena told her that she had a past in Ireland that needed clearing. Then she proceeded to recount events in Kelly's present-day life that were directly related to the past life. Helena is a very gifted seer and even tuned into an uncle that she was sure would help Kelly pay for the trip.

I'm thrilled that a friend will be joining me on this next journey. More importantly, the plan to go to Ireland brings immediate relief from my rage.

Chapter 4
Journey to the
Stone Circles

The ancient Celts call to me. I hear their voices carried by the wind over the vast ocean, emerging from the mist and enveloping me with their alluring songs. They are the stone people, standing tall atop a field of green, anchoring the past, and holding open the portal to the future. Spirals of the Triple Goddess deeply engraved in stone, standing the test of time. I crawl beneath an old grove of gnarled oaks and sing a song to the Mother Goddess, awakening her from her slumber. It's me, I whisper. I've returned to you. I'm remembering you as I stir awake the forgotten life within me.

Navigating a precarious, rocky footpath, we follow Helena down to a narrow strip of shore just north of the Cliffs of Moher. It's the only section where the water doesn't directly meet the cliffs' edge. The beach is rough with shards of shale and sandstone and seaweed strewn about.

"This is one of the thin places of Ireland," Helena shouts over the booming sound of the waves crashing on cliffs as we near the tempestuous waters. It's breathtaking, with razor-edged cliffs that are impressively tall and stand facing the mighty Atlantic Ocean.

She instructs us to do a meditation with a partner. Kelly and I catch each other's glances and I nod, pointing in a direction that is far from the others. We settle into a place surrounded by a few, large boulders where the risk of a rising tide is minimal. With Kelly standing across from me, we hold hands while hearing the waves crash behind us and scramble to the shore. The cool, ocean mist infused with the heady smell of drying seaweed clinging to the nearby rocks, caresses my skin. It's the smell of family vacations. After a few giggles, we close our eyes. I feel the warmth of her hands in mine and hear the call of seagulls overhead. Eventually, I slip into a deep meditation.

I see myself in a dark, hooded cape that's weathered and worn. I'm standing with another woman with long auburn hair. She feels like Kelly, even though she looks nothing like her. We're both surrounded by a group of children in another time and place, like a school. Some children at play in a garden enclosed by a primitive fence made with rocks and bent tree saplings. Others appear to be spinning as I see piles of raw wool and what looks like drop spindles in their hands. Sheep graze in a nearby pasture. Much like the dream I had.

Dread and apprehension well up inside of me. Pulling my hands away, I open my eyes not wanting to see anymore but can't escape the feeling of doom. I look at Kelly searching for answers.

"What did you see?" she asks with concern.

I share with her my image of the two of us and the children.

"Yeah, I had the same image!" she exclaims, wide eyed.

"Did you feel there's more to the story?"

"I don't know, I didn't really feel anything else. Why?" she asks.

"Not sure, but I have a sick feeling in my stomach," I say, fighting back waves of nausea. "I'm just going to be with it and see how it unfolds."

Before leaving, I turn to the vast ocean, watching the waves crash against the rocks, spraying mist that glistens in the sunlight. The Mother Goddess is so palpable here. I want to let go of the dread I'm feeling, dive deep into her waters and surrender myself to her, but the water is frigid, and the rest of the group is already heading back to the bus.

I understand what Helena means by it being a "thin place." The veil that separates us from the Sidhe (*pronounced shee*), or the faerie world, is more transparent here in Ireland. Perhaps it's because the Irish have kept the connection between humans and the Sidhe alive through their myths and stories and poetry. Or maybe because Ireland is an island with countless mountains and valleys, it's easy for the Sidhe to stay hidden, without completely disappearing.

I wake the next morning, still with slight nausea and dread. The bus driver, Mick, takes our small group through the winding roads of the Irish countryside.

We pass a small stone circle, barely visible from the road. I turn just in time to get a glimpse. Its presence tugs at me, but for some reason I say nothing. We continue for about two miles down the road when I hear Helena yell.

"Stop the bus!"

Mick pulls over to the side of the road, shaking his head at Helena's sudden command.

"We missed it. It's back there somewhere," says Helena.

"What do you mean it's back there? We didn't see anything!" exclaims Mick.

"No, no, it's back there. We went past it. I can feel it," Helena says as she waves her arms in the direction behind us.

Rolling his eyes, and in his Irish accent, Mick says, "Good God, woman. Don't you use a map or directions? What do you mean you feel it?"

"I feel it. It's there. Just turn the bus around," Helena says defiantly.

I chuckle to myself. I love Helena's confidence when it comes to her intuition, and I love watching her and Mick's interactions. They bicker like an old married couple.

I don't feel like laughing, though, as a feeling of dread comes over me when Mick pulls our bus over to the side of the road. I can see the stone circle at the very top of the hill. Careful not to brush against the thick patch of stinging nettles growing at the edge of the field, we follow the well-worn footpath up the hill, past clumps of mugwort and flowering trefoil. Reaching the crest, I feel close to the clouds, far from the Irish bogs. I look past the stone circle and sweeping green landscape. Beyond, is a view of the sea, a small cove with cliffs descending down to the shore. I gasp, and quickly turn back to count the stones in the stone circle. *This is the place in my dreams.* Helena takes out her copper dowsing rods and walks to the center of the stone circle. The rods swing wildly, then cross becoming completely still, revealing the exact center of the stone circle and its powerful vortex.

I decide to lie down right over the vortex thinking it will help bring up whatever is making me feel nauseous. I lay face down on the hard ground, noticing a clump of red clover nearby that looks dry and windswept. A few minutes pass, when suddenly my nausea worsens. I think for sure I'm going to throw up. I want to run away, but the rage contained in my belly stirs. A past-life story unfolds. I see an army of Roman soldiers invading, children screaming and running everywhere. I'm wearing a long, hooded cape, and don't know where to turn, how to keep the children safe from the sudden storm of soldiers. The images are like a thousand daggers piercing my heart. I sob with anguish over the brutal scene. No other outcome is possible other than complete annihilation. Rage quickly turns to grief unearthed. I lay sobbing, uncontrollably. It all happened so quickly.

The other women in the group hurry over and circle around me. They lift me off the ground, cradling me, as they sing a song to help me release my pain. I feel raw and empty. It's a strange feeling to let go of grief. Native Americans have said that those who are grieving are closer to God and that's how I feel in this moment. I carry no protection having made my peace with loss — no more holding onto what once was. The rage contained in my belly is gone. The hills in the distance appear brighter and the sea far below sparkles like a million little diamonds as the sun shines down. The beauty washes through me like a healing balm to my soul. I feel the protective, bright green mantle of Brigid around my shoulders. I bend down, placing my hands on the ground, blessing the land and the lives lost with my tears before our group slowly makes our way back to the bus. My dreams over the past several months of a goddess culture coupled with growing rage, now all make sense.

"How are you feeling?" Kelly asks as she sits down next to me.

"I feel much better, a little wiped out, emotionally. Empty in a good way," I say.

"Yeah, I bet," she says as we both turned to listen to Helena.

"We're stopping up ahead for a little while. There's a woman selling hand-knit sweaters on the side of the road," Helena announces to everyone.

This is exactly what I need. The old woman's weathered cart sits on the edge of the road. It's filled with sweaters hanging and others neatly folded and stacked, all natural shades of the sheep themselves.

"Hi! You have gorgeous sweaters. Did you knit all these?" I ask the smiling, older woman sitting next to her cart.

"Aye, I did. They're knit from the wool right off of me own sheep. Me farm is right over the hill. That there are smalls, at the end over there," she says, pointing to the other side of her cart.

Being a knitter myself, I appreciate the fine craftsmanship of the hand-knit sweaters and the Aran designs so meticulously woven into each sweater.

Mary Flanagan's roadside cart of Irish-knit sweaters takes my mind off the earlier events and holds our group captive for over an hour as we all try on sweaters.

"I'll take this one," I say, handing my money to the woman. I put the heather-brown sweater on over my t-shirt before returning to the bus. The smell of lanolin and the Irish countryside is woven into each stitch. I appreciate the added warmth, but even more so, its protection while still feeling so raw.

Over the next few days, I feel the presence of an ancient goddess pulling at my roots like a heavy anchor. I imagine it's an Cailleach, the Celtic name given to winter's old hag — a goddess of great antiquity. Each day brings yet another dismantling — an upheaval of emotions that brings me closer to her.

I wake the next morning with an uneasy feeling and peer through the small window of the quaint B&B where we arrived late last evening. A thick layer of fog blankets the streets of the small, English village, with ominous clouds hanging low overhead. The weather matches my mood, and I slowly climb out from underneath the cozy down comforter, slip on my jeans, my new, cozy sweater and hiking boots before meeting the group for breakfast.

After several cups of tea, black pudding and cranberry scones, we climb aboard our small bus, this time with a new driver named Harry. He greets each one of us with a cheery smile. We wind our way through the village streets and out into the countryside. We follow a tree-lined, dirt road that reminds me so much of our roads back home, and I find comfort in its familiarity.

Soon, Harry pulls over to the side of the road.

"We're visiting Long Meg, Britain's largest stone circle," shouts Helena over the pounding rain. "The folklore says that Long Meg and her daughters were once a coven of witches who were turned to stone by a wizard named Michael Scot of Scotland."

I get off the bus and stand in the cold, soaking rain that quickly permeates my coat and leaves my hair dripping. I follow Helena and the rest of the group out into an expansive field that overlooks the villages below, still hidden by dense fog and low-laying clouds.

We gather in a circle amidst the stones, singing and dancing. I'm lost in the sound of our melodic voices and the rain pitter pattering on my coat. I close my eyes and see with my inner vision, the face of a skinny, gaunt looking woman. I shudder and open my eyes as a way to avoid what I see. I close my eyes again and the face reappears, this time uglier and I turn away, frustrated.

She appears once again, this time looking like she just stepped off the stage of a horror movie with pasty white skin and glowing red eyes. I realize that turning away from her is only making her appear worse. So, I turn to her, and feel a woman, an aspect of myself, right behind me. Her arms reach through mine to the hideous face I don't want to look at. She's there to show me how to embrace my shadow.

"Don't turn away, don't turn away," she instructs.

I resign myself to "her" commands and look deep into the red eyes of the pale-faced woman. So much love flows through me, a fierce and fearless power. My embrace melts all the ugliness away, until, in front of me stands a beautiful woman, with fine, delicate features. Her pale skin turns to rosy, pink flesh, her straggly hair to a beautiful, silky mane and her red eyes of fury turn to deep pools of sapphire.

I feel humbled and shy from this powerful moment as though the Goddess is witnessing more of me than I dare reveal. Everyone else in the group is still dancing and singing. My body joins in, but

WHEN THE DARK MOTHER CALLS

I'm still in-between worlds. Beyond the women in our group, I see the stones, the daughters of Long Meg dancing with us.

I can't run from my shadow, otherwise, my shadow will run my life.

After a long drive north, adorable little puffins stand on the shoreline welcoming us to the Orkney islands as our ferry makes its way across the northern waters of the Atlantic. We arrive at our place by the sea, a beautiful, old stone house with lots of pathways winding through gardens and under wobbly, wooden archways. We remain on the bus while Helena goes in to tell the innkeeper we've arrived. I can tell Helena is keeping her fingers crossed that each place will remember her reservations made months ago.

The Orkneys is like entering the shadow itself. With little light for many months, the deep earthiness of this island is very detectable. Helena has traveled to the Orkneys frequently and tells us, before arriving on the island, that it beckons the shadow to come out of hiding. I watch her standing taller, as if strengthening her core, preparing for the onset of drama or at the very least, unsettledness amongst our group members.

As Helena has anticipated, within hours of arriving on the island, some of our group members are irritable resulting in a few squabbles and complaints. I'm dealing with my own shadow on the rise. Feelings of unexplained jealousy envelope me like a dark cloud, and I retreat to a bench in a small unkept garden. Remembering what I learned the day before at Long Meg, I imagine a young woman, an aspect of myself raging with jealousy. I sit and listen like a good friend or a mother would with an angry child. The more I listen and hold the feelings of jealousy with love, the more the feelings soften, and the dark cloud dissipates. Beneath jealousy is my fear of being unloveable. A wound from my marriage that still bleeds. I am painfully aware of my past relationships with men that left me broken-hearted. I've had the habit of falling in love with a man's potential, ignoring the reality of how he actually shows up. I want to shed tears, but my eyes remain dry, and my heart closed, not ready to release the pain.

Later, Helena holds a council. I'm unsure as to what transpired prior to our council, but it's apparent that something occurred between a few of our group members.

"Don't judge the shadow work of others. We have all been there," Helena says with furrowed brow. "We have all played the role of the aggressor whether it was this lifetime or another. We all come full circle having played both roles in EVERY dynamic," she says, waving her finger in the air, further demonstrating her fierceness.

It's a brief council, and I'm still unclear as to what happened, but it's apparent her words penetrate everyone in the group. Whatever edge may have existed prior is gone, and the energy of the group softens.

Helena's words stuck with me. Judgment has sharp edges. I think back to a time when I came face to face with my own judgement while stopped at the traffic light in our nearby town. I saw a man walking on the street with soiled clothes and missing teeth. He wasn't a homeless man, just not tended to. I didn't want to feel judgment, but I did. As I watched him, I saw his higher self right behind him turn to me and smile brightly. He said, "I chose this experience so I could further learn compassion." I remember feeling so exposed and humbled, and all judgement dropped away.

Later, in the evening, we have a delicious dinner of roast lamb, fresh scallops, and haggis, some of Orkney's specialties. With our stomachs full, we gather around the fireplace, relaxing with cups of hot tea and honey as Helena shares stories about the mysteries of Orkney. We're waiting to board our bus and drive to the Ring of Brodgar for a midnight ceremony, a well-known, Neolithic henge and stone circle northeast of Stromness.

"It's special among the ancient sites," Helena explains in a low voice, careful not to disturb other guests staying at the B&B. "Because, like Avebury and Stonehenge, it has both a stone circle and henge, large, earthen banks. Some researchers have estimated it to be 6000 years old. The interesting part is the builders of this site used the same techniques to measure the sky as did the Egyptians."

We continue the conversation once on the bus. "Who were the builders?" many of us ask. "Legends speak of a race of giants, some say an ancient priesthood, and others speculate the star beings," answers Helena.

As we arrive, there is just enough light to make out the giant stones off in the distance. Silhouetted against the dark blue, star-filled sky, they look like ancient Druids in assembly, anchored in stillness at the edge of the world, and mysteriously stern. My heart beats faster with a wave of excitement. A different experience than with the other stone circles.

We leave Harry behind as we climb the tor, following a narrow footpath illuminated only by the light of the moon. Walking in a procession around the outside of the stone circle, in a counter-clockwise direction, we open the energetic doorway before entering.

Wearing a woolen cape with a scarf draped over her head, Helena looks like an ancient priestess from another time and place. She takes her role as guide and initiator very seriously. Each step she takes is purposeful, and I can tell by the way she's holding her arms, with her right arm up with hand open and her left pointing down to the ground, that she's working with the energy of the place. It's the same hand positioning I see on the images of the magician in the traditional Tarot card decks.

A tall, erect stone grips my attention jolting me awake to the notion that the stones are indeed alive. Taking note of where the stone stands, I finish opening the door with the others. The night air is cool, and the fine mist begins to move in from the waters that surround Orkney. The pungent odor of peat bog and heather that grow clustered across the island, interwoven with the smell of fresh salt water is intoxicating. The mist clings to my face and hair, turning my otherwise straight locks into a wild and curly mane.

Our circle of women disperse as each goes to explore the stone circle and meditate on their own. I head to the standing stone that previously caught my attention. With arms spread wide, I lean against the stone. I detect a male presence within the stone, and a warm sensuality begins to rise, inviting my hips to sway back and forth. My heart opens, and my body softens like a spring rain thawing the frozen ground. Passion and desire wake up inside of me that I haven't felt in a long time. In the distance, I hear the faint, bubbling call of the curlew floating through the air. I press my cheek against the cold, damp stone. It smells like an evocative blend of both earth and sea.

I think back to a passage I read in one of the books on stone circles I had borrowed from the library a few months back. *Stone circles are portals where the human and the faerie meet. Here, amongst the stones, our worlds meld as one and together we can dance, make love and create children that carry both human and faerie blood.*

What feels like only a few minutes has been over an hour and so I say goodbye and join the rest of the group to close the circle.

We return to the bus to find Harry sitting at the wheel, white as a ghost.

"Harry, what's wrong?" asks Helena.

"I don't want to talk about it," he snaps, fingers clutching the steering wheel until his knuckles turn white. Helena looks back at the group and shrugs, letting it drop.

We return to our lodging for the night. I lay in bed, enveloped in heavy layers of wool blankets and flannel sheets, feeling into the night and the mysteries of the deep earth energy that infuses the Island of Orkney. I still feel the masculine presence from the stone with me. It feels unexplainably familiar, and I bask in the energy wondering if this is a person I will soon meet or my faerie counterpart.

Kelly and our roommate, Gloria, are sound asleep. Cool air finds its way between the cracks of the old stone house. While something deep stirs inside me, something ancient awakens from the shadowy depths of the island like reaching into a cauldron and pulling out a seed of life buried in the loamy earth. The aphotic landscape acts as a gateway for reaching far into the void and awakening the dreaming self.

Pulling the covers over my chilled shoulders, my thoughts wander to the evening's ceremony and the masculine presence. I've been in survival mode since I left my marriage two years ago, attending to the details of the move, finding a home, and making sure the kids have what they need. It feels good to let my guard down, momentarily, and open to a more sensual way of being. I drift into a deep sleep.

Morning comes too soon, and the three of us drag ourselves out of bed and quickly put on our clothes to keep warm. A hearty breakfast of hot oatmeal and dried fruit is waiting for us in the sunroom. Helena invites anyone who wants to share their experience from the stone circle, to do so. Surprisingly, Harry, still shook, speaks up.

"After you all had been up on the hill for quite some time, I decided to stroll on up and see how you were all getting on. I couldn't see any of you, so walked around for a bit. Before I knew it, I was so disoriented, I had no idea what direction the bus was in. I saw a tall gentleman wearing a long, dark trench coat, so I walked towards him and asked him how to get back to the bus. He told me which direction to walk while pointing with his hand. I turned to thank him, and what had been a man giving me directions, was a tall stone."

This is clearly the first mystical experience that Harry has ever had, and it scared him. He spoke in a very controlled manner, but we can tell by his wide eyes that he is really shaken by this experience.

"Harry, that must have been very scary for you. The stones are magical, and we can see them in many different ways. You're okay," Helena says in her softest voice. Harry seems to feel better just being able to share his experience with us, trusting we'd understand.

After a few days exploring the Orkneys, we head south to the western shores of Scotland. The old Scottish sea captain that steers our boat safely to the shores of Iona is a character right out of a movie. His wild salt and pepper hair, long beard, sea-weathered face and thick, gruff Scottish accent accompany us on the final leg of our journey, the tiny, magical island of Iona. A place of the heart.

As I see the small island in the distance, I remember a book I read over the winter on the Grail mysteries. It spoke of many legends of Iona connecting it to not only the Arthurian legends, but Atlantis as well. Some speak of a small group of men and women who began an Atlantean colony on Iona, referring to it as "a distant place of the heart." Other legends speak of a group of priestesses inhabiting Iona who referred to themselves as the Priestesses of Ank, or Sacred Well of Life. This is so similar to the Egyptian Ankh, which is a symbol of eternal life and Divine union and makes me wonder what the connection is between the two lands. Some believe the priestesses were the basis to the legendary Lady of the Lake, who offers healing and renewal to the psyche of man. Others tell stories of Mary Magdalene having stayed on the island, giving birth to Jesus' last son, John Martinus. So many legends attributed to this tiny island, and I feel myself slip into a sense of timelessness.

We arrive on the shore and walk down the cobblestone street dragging our luggage behind us. There's little here, but the medieval abbey and a couple small inns for visitors. It feels peaceful, a stillness that I haven't felt in many places. Leaving my unpacked bags in my small, cozy room with a view of the sea, I take the time before dinner to wander around the island. I follow a well-worn foot path that takes me over the hill, past old stone walls that keep the grazing sheep within their pasture. I eventually come to a beautiful, sandy beach.

I sit down, enjoying the pristine stretch of white sand and colorful stones, the rising waves crashing to the shore and the hills just behind me dotted with white sheep. My thoughts drift to my ex-husband. It's been just over 2 years since I left. I've been so busy getting things in order, making sure the kids were settled in from our move, that I haven't taken the time to grieve.

With my inner vision, I see images of him moving on. I sense he's beginning a new relationship, the knowing descends on me like a cloud. I'm relieved to be out of the marriage, and at the same time, deeply sad. All my hopes and dreams of being married, having a family, living happily ever after have fallen apart.

I stay present with the sadness, not wanting to let myself off the hook from feeling the pain. My heart aches as though it wants to break open, to let go of all the grief I've unknowingly held onto. Eventually, like a beaver's dam giving way to the pressure of the water, my sadness spills forth as deep sobs. My tears aren't for the loss of him, but more for the loss of my dreams. Growing up, I had imagined a very traditional life, handsome husband, beautiful home, children and a dog by my side. My life is taking a completely different turn that I don't understand. I love everything I'm learning with Helena but have no idea where it's leading me, and I grieve for the life I let go of.

Looking around to see if I am alone, I take off my clothes and toss them on a nearby rock. I quickly plunge into the cold sea. I feel more naked than I'm comfortable with. Physically naked as well as emotionally. The water holds me, gently rocking me by its undulating current as I release my final tears. *How many other women before me shed their tears in this sea?* An image of women throughout time comes to me as I watch them, one by one, step into the swelling seas off the shores of Iona, naked, crumpled over, grieving, giving in to their pain, their losses, their disappointments. Dreams that took a sudden detour leaving them without any solid footing, a free fall into the arms of the Mother.

The gentle current carries me back to the shore. Wet, salty and cold, I slip on my jeans and t-shirt and lay in the sand caressed by the warm rays of the sun. My heart feels free from the burden of grief. I pick up two small stones that are cool to the touch and place them over my swollen eyes.

Later in the evening, we finish an incredible meal of locally grown lamb roast, with rosemary and island grown vegetables. All through the meal, my chest is tight and becomes increasingly uncomfortable, despite releasing grief earlier in the day. As Helena gets ready to retire for the evening, I run to catch her.

"Helena, can I check in with you before you go to bed?" I ask.

"Of course, sweetie, what is it?" she responds with a concerned look on her face.

"I'm feeling something right here," I say pointing to my chest. "It feels really tight, like something wants to come out."

Helena puts her hand on my chest and tunes in.

"Hmmm, there's a stone, a planetary stone that was put in your field for you to find your ex-husband in this lifetime."

She pushes her hand into my chest as though retrieving an actual stone from my heart. Strangely, her words make sense to me, and I imagine some sort of magnet that drew me to him.

"Ahhh, there it goes. Feel better?" she asks.

"Uhhh, yeah, much better! Thank you!" I say giving her a hug.

"Well, you've done the work. You found him, you had the kids you were supposed to have together and now it's complete. Good work!" She smiles knowingly, and we say good night.

My chest feels open and clear, no more tightness. Even though I have no interest whatsoever in meeting a man, I feel perhaps I can love again.

As I lie in bed, inhaling the salt-water breeze that blows in from my opened window, I think about the stone and Helena's words. *A planetary stone to find my ex-husband.* A memory surfaces — a message I heard loud and clear just weeks after Matthew was born. I was in our bedroom gathering the laundry, and heard a voice in my head say, "You need to have one more child with him and then you will leave." I was horrified hearing this message that, at the time, I heard as my own thought. I was baffled and scolded myself for having such an awful thought as a young wife and mother. But now I wonder about the connection between the stone in my chest and this message. It's a mysterious puzzle. I think of the role of the priestesses who carried forth the royal bloodline. Not a royal lineage that we think of in regard to England's kings, but a king of a different sort — the royal bloodline that carries the DNA from both human and the Sidhe, weaving its way through history like a grapevine weaves its way through the forest. Perhaps there's a greater purpose to my first marriage and the children we have together.

It's difficult for me to pull myself out of this journey, away from the power of the stone circles and back into the world. Sitting in the airport waiting for my flight to return home, I watch the people hurrying by with their luggage in tow. Their world is muffled and feels faraway. I can still smell the heather and the salt air. The weight of the goddess like a heavy anchor. The power of the stone circles that called to me months prior. I left so much here.

A mom walks by, holding the hands of her two young children. The children both look my way, and our eyes meet. I smile. Our momentary connection pulls me into the here and now. My heart aches to return home and be with my children. And as I imagine seeing their sweet faces greeting me at the airport, the stone circles fade into the abyss. I no longer feel pulled in any other direction but home.

Chapter 5
A Vision Birthed

*L*ike *a tree's buds in spring, a potent life force becomes too great to contain. They become swollen until finally giving way to life, growth — the actualization of potential.*

"Find the prettiest ones and we'll take them back to the house." The kids and I walk through the woods in our backyard looking for the prettiest and brightest colored leaves. This Fall brings such a symphony of colors. The hills that surround us are lit up in all their glory, like a regal parade of kings and queens donned in their robes of gold, red, orange and pink. We make our way through the old, deciduous forest enjoying the earthy smell of the leaves rustling beneath our feet, the slight chill in the air and Bradford, our dog, leading the way with his tail wagging.

Life slows down this time of year, with shorter days and colder nights, and my focus shifts to home and hearth, making sure we have wood for the winter and pulling our down comforters out from the old cedar chest. I especially love the inward pull of this time of year. Like the trees, I descend into my own roots for nourishment with anticipation of the winter months to come.

As I watch the colorful leaves drift to the ground, I think how natural a process it is to let go of what no longer serves us. The natural cycle of death and rebirth that's an integral part of our experience living on earth. I let go of so much during my last trip — the grief of a tremendous loss that felt as old as the stones.

We return home with our basket of leaves just in time for me to take a loaf of bread out of the oven. There's nothing that feels like home more than the sweet smell of homemade bread baking. I slice a few pieces and spread them with butter and honey and carry them over to the table where the kids are anxiously waiting. I light a candle in honor of the goddess and Samhain. My own quiet honoring for just the three of us, while my heart remembers lively festivals once shared.

I sit at our kitchen table, looking at my decor. It's apparent that I've been living a borrowed life. My home is decorated in a colonial theme, but where am I? It no longer represents me, and I want to tear down the curtains and the Grandma Moses paintings and replace them with something that portrays who I am becoming. I'm shedding my old self like the trees letting go of their old leaves.

My trip to the British Isles grounded me. I no longer feel the mounting frustration and rage that consumed me just before the trip. The dismantling process I'd undergone tore away my beliefs along with the old patriarchal form. I cleared the way to build a life more aligned with the Goddess, but honestly, don't know where to begin. I feel like a tiny bird, sitting atop a tall oak. In every direction, I see a world I don't belong in.

Now and then, as I drift off to sleep, I think back to the sensual experience at the Brodgar Stone Circle in the Orkneys, but I can't quite give in or surrender to the flow of my feminine energy. I want to, but I'm still in survival mode since my divorce. It hasn't been easy to play the role of both mother and father and taking time for myself to bask in the glow of my sensuality feels like a luxury I can't afford. So, I keep moving forward, making sure the kids have what they need.

I pour much of my energy and focus into creating home school programs for children. My displeasure with the public school continues, and I decide to create my own school. I can't erase the memories that surfaced on the trip of a different way of learning — the old ways that we lost thousands of years ago.

Today's world, in comparison, is a strange, harsh overlay, like a blanket put over a fire, smothering its flame until it's completely extinguished. It's the world of the patriarch silencing the feminine, shoving her underground. I think this is why I crave a school environment that fosters the children's natural gifts, cultivates their intuition and imagination, and instills a sense of the world beyond the physical realm. I want to give the kids a different experience and at the same time, heal my own school experience.

I spend the winter months putting together ideas and creating curriculum for children's programs. As the vision for the school comes to life, it feels like a quickening, the first stirrings of life the mother feels inside her belly. By the time spring comes, I'm ready to give birth to my vision while Kelly's giving birth to her second child. I'm with her when her son is born into the world and later, she's my spiritual midwife. She patiently sits and listens to me as I talk about one idea after another while preparing to host a community gathering. As the time nears, my throat swells almost shut. Despite taking herbs and vitamin C, the swelling lasts for weeks.

One day, Kelly and I are out shopping. My throat nearly closes and is so painful. I pull the car over to the side of the road. I need to figure out what's going on. I'm birthing a vision and my throat's the birth canal. Kelly asks me questions like a midwife gently assisting in pulling out the baby. While trying to relax and breathe through the closing passageway, I answer her questions as I dig deep inside, into my feelings. My body remembers the destruction of the mystery schools and the killing of the priestesses, the whole event that was unveiled back in Ireland in the center of the stone circle. My swollen throat is evidence to my resistance to opening up and letting go. It's like what I imagine a mother would feel birthing a child into a turbulent world. Am I birthing the vision or myself? Maybe they're one in the same.

Am I safe? That's the question that remains unanswered. I feel danger revealing both myself and my vision of another way of living. Images of being scorned, betrayed while a warrior's sword pierces my heart leaving me drenched in my own pool of blood. My body shakes with fear. Eventually, my heart can no longer hold the shackles of the past. Tears erupt carrying both my fear and grief to the surface. As I find the courage to verbalize my fears my body eventually relaxes. My throat opens like the softening of a woman's vagina as the baby is born. The swelling completely disappears. While the fear lessens, it never completely goes away, but I learn to walk with it, befriend it and not let it control me.

Chapter 6

The Sword of Truth

My voice, once bound to the persona of the nice, polite girl, now escapes its place of hiding, breaking free from the fears that have kept me silent for so many years.

There's something to it when you reach a new level of awareness and consciousness, the energy seems to attract new people and new experiences. Shortly after my "birthing" experience, I receive a call from a man who introduces himself as a geomancer, one that studies the ley lines of the earth.

He seems to know all about my vision despite the fact I've never met him. He and his geomancer group have mapped out the northeast with particular points of power that reveals a place, similar to a sacred site. I can't get a straight answer out of him as to how he knows anything about me or even how he found my phone number. I'm interested in what he's saying, just not in the way he's saying it. He discloses only bits of information while inferring so much more. I feel like he's baiting me and then pulling away the bait when I ask questions.

A few days later, one of his friends calls me to arrange a meeting. I feel a connection with him, somewhat of an attraction while we talk on the phone but meeting him in person is a different story. I invite Kelly and her family over for dinner, in part to meet him, but also for my own comfort. As we sit around the dinner table, partaking in casual conversation, I become more unsettled. Any attraction that I previously felt quickly disappears. He acts smug and inconsiderate, and several times he makes comments as though he knows something about me that I have yet to discover. It feels like an attempt to establish control. I'm guarded the entire evening, and when Wendy, my cat jumps up on his lap and randomly bites him, I know it's time for him to leave.

The next morning, I wake with a really high fever. Very rarely do I get sick with fevers and neither of the kids have been sick. I send them across the road to my parent's house as I lie on the couch drenched in sweat, taking small sips of water. Every time I close my eyes, I see something writhing inside of me like a snake, not the ally I've come to know and revere. It doesn't feel good, and I question whether I'm being psychically attacked. I don't really understand at that time what it even means, but these are the words that come to me. My mom stops in to check on me and sits next to the couch laying cold compresses on my forehead. Bradford won't leave my side and keeps licking my feet at the other end of the couch. After my mom leaves, I muster up enough strength to get to the phone. I call Helena.

Helena listens intently to my story. Oddly, she hadn't felt well the night before so she's very keen on hearing what I have to say. Helena and I have known each other for four years now. Our connection is strong. We both know we've traveled lifetimes together as wise women. I tell her about the two men, the one who had initially called me and the one who came to visit.

"What do you think about them?" I ask. Helena, being clairvoyant and a very clear seer and psychic is great at reading people from afar. She starts to answer and then stops.

"What do YOU think?" she asks me.

I teeter on the edge of what feels like a cliff — my nice girl persona scrambles to find the appropriate answer while my truth burns hot in my belly. I'm so used to giving answers that make others happy, that are acceptable, kind and compassionate. Yet, I can no longer deny my truth aligned with the Goddess. She holds little regard for niceties and pleasantries. She's not afraid to feel, to speak her mind, to contradict.

"Well…, they seem knowledgeable when it comes to geomancy. And they seem to be in tune with the vision I've been carrying," I say feeling a deep inner conflict as I carefully choose my words.

She stops me and asks, "But do you like them?"

I pause, my mind races through the countless pages of my life's book, *How to be Nice and Liked by Everyone*. Then finally, the dam breaks and I blurt out, "No, I hate them! They're arrogant, inconsiderate, egotistical and they sneer."

To speak from such a deep truth, bypassing any kind of domesticated bullshit answer, feels so incredibly freeing. It isn't easy for me to speak my truth much less even know my truth. I remember back to a time when I was three years old and getting so furious over something my brother was doing and wouldn't stop. I don't remember what it was, but it was a harmless big brother and little sister situation. In that moment I got really angry and threw a pen. I remember the shocked look of fear in my mother's and brother's eyes. I perceived their reaction as though my anger was bad and needed to be kept tucked away. So, over the years, I kept my anger at bay and the "nice girl" took over.

Helena is silent on the other end of the phone. I imagine she's either smiling to herself or rolling her eyes over how long it took me to get to the down and dirty truth of the matter.

She then says, "I agree. So, what are you going to do about it?"

Another hurdle. It's not enough for me to speak my truth. How am I going to stand in my truth? I feel nauseous, and my heart beats in my throat. The past life story from Ireland once again comes alive and the men feel like the Roman soldiers storming my life. No visible armor, or shields and swords, but the same aggressive energy. I want to run and hide, retreat from the situation, but know I can't.

I see the truth like a morning fog slowly dissipating as the sun rises. And the more I see the truth, the stronger I feel. My fever diminishes and I know I need to take action, stand my ground and protect my vision as I would my own child.

I call the man who initially contacted me. He answers the phone, but upon discovering it's me on the other end, his voice shifts from a benevolent tone to a pompous inflection. I tell him that I don't care for his or his friend's way of going about business and prefer they don't contact me again. He asks me a few questions pertaining to the work I'm doing with creating a school and community. I tell him I have no desire to share any of my thoughts with him and hang up the phone.

My strength drains from me as soon as I hang up, and my body trembles with fear. I go outdoors and lay down on the cool ground. The earthy smell of Fall leaves and the warmth of the sun helps me to relax. I feel like a returning priestess, reclaiming myself and the Goddess culture in a new era, absent of medieval peril. It reminds me of a scene in a movie where the one who has been betrayed, gathers their strength, formulates their strategy and returns to take back what is rightfully theirs.

As I lie in the grass and close my eyes, an image of a gleaming sword comes to me, suspended in midair. I speak the words, *The Sword of Truth*. It has a power all its own, an undeniable strength. I had some knowledge of the grail mysteries and intuitively knew it had something to do with the Excalibur, the legendary sword belonging to King Arthur. It holds the power of polarity and separates the old so the new can be birthed. It requires standing in your truth and the willingness to sever ties with what no longer serves you. The sword's strength is passed onto the one who wields it. And the one is chosen only by the Goddess herself.

This is a threshold moment for me. Before meeting Helena and starting this journey, I would have either dismissed my feelings of the two men and ignored them or tolerated their behavior. But I can't do that now. I feel my voice is speaking for thousands of women who have been wronged in past situations and had their way of living taken from them. In this moment, I become my own authority and stop giving my power over to others who I feel know more. It reminds me of a moment shortly after giving birth to my first child. My mom was staying at our house to help, and I questioned whether I'd be as good of a mom as she was. I watched her tend to my baby's needs and observed my own thoughts as I put her in the position of complete authority on child rearing. Fortunately, my mama bear rose up, counteracting my thoughts and claimed my own instinctual nature and authority as a new mom. In a way, I am again, claiming my own authority when it comes to the vision I'm birthing.

My thoughts wander back to a few years earlier when I was living in New Hampshire. I joined a group that was working with Clarissa Pinkola Estes book, *Running with the Wolves.* Her book had just hit the shelves of bookstores. Reading her stories was a soothing balm to my soul. My psyche was starving for the archetypal stories and images conveyed in her book and I inhaled her words as though I had been deprived of oxygen. They flung open the doors to my inner world, a landscape I had yet to discover. In the group, we were instructed to draw a self-portrait. I drew my face, my long hair, a blouse, a skirt and a strand of pearls. As I began to draw my legs, the feet of a wolf emerged. I then drew a long wolf's tail and furry ears coming out of the top of my head.

Now, several years later, I drop the pearls and the domesticated self, finally revealing my wild nature.

A few weeks later, I wake, startled from a dream. I quickly search my bedroom for anything familiar. I can just make out the shape of my dresser and the glow of the moon outside my window. *Okay, just a dream.* Yet my heart is beating fast, and I can't shake the fear. Jessi had, at some point in the middle of the night, climbed in bed with me, something that was becoming a nightly routine. I gently pick up her tiny arm that is flung across my chest, being careful not to wake her, and slide out of bed wrapping my knitted shawl over my chilled arms. The full moon casts an eerie shadow across the lawn, and I peer out the window searching for answers and recalling the details of my dream.

I run down an old cobblestone street frantically looking over my shoulder. I hear fast approaching footsteps behind me. Up ahead, I see an unobtrusive-looking cathedral. Running to the heavy, wooden doors, I rattle the wrought-iron latch. It creaks open, and I slip into the darkness, quickly closing the door behind me. I hide in the dark corner, beneath an oak table laden with books. I'm concealed by the shadows, breathing heavily, tucking my knees up to my chest, covered by a thick, wool cape trying to make myself as small as possible.

I wrap my shawl tighter, trying to ease the fear that ripples through me. As I peer out the window, into the moonlit sky, I hear the word "France."

Another trip, so soon?

It hasn't been quite a year since I got back from the British Isles, and I resist the message.

"I'm not going. Besides, I don't think I have the money to go anyways. And it's too soon to leave the kids again." I'm speaking to the Goddess herself and holding the posture of a stubborn child with my arms crossed and feet firmly planted.

Strong in my convictions, there was another part of me saying, "You know you're going. You know everything will work out. This is part of your path. It will be okay."

I walk across the hall and peek into Matthew's room. He's sound asleep with Bradford snoring next to him. I creep back into bed, slowly pulling at the covers. Feeling the warmth of my daughter's little body, I slide my arm over her, pulling her close.

This is my continual path of initiation. My actions, my moments of truth, my times of confronting fear and overcoming struggles set the next initiation into motion. Unlike our ancient ancestors who used to create initiatory experiences by burying the initiate underground or having them cross a narrow bridge lined with crocodiles on either side, I rely on my life's experiences to initiate me.

Everyday life is giving me the opportunities to grow, to expand and to become more of who I am, to discover my power, to stand in my truth. To be initiated. To turn away from these moments, would be to turn away from myself. I know I can't do that.

The Cauldron

Initiation by Water

*The Cauldron, the Cup or also known as the grail is one of the
oldest known symbols. It's a vessel that relates to the element of
water. Many traditions depict a goddess stirring a cauldron —
she is the goddess of death and rebirth. The cauldron is where the
alchemical process of transformation takes place.*

*In life, we have challenges and situations that leave us
emotionally raw where neither strength nor strategy bring resolve.
We have no choice but to surrender to the strong emotions being
evoked and fall into the goddess' cauldron to be made anew. Loss
does this. Betrayal does this. We surrender to a force far greater
and are forever changed. We are shaped by this initiation for
we now understand the pain of the human experience. We are
imbued with wisdom and compassion for the pains of humanity.
The magical cauldron comes to us once we've fully surrendered
and holds the wisdom gained and the life-giving
waters of renewal.*

The cauldron is what keeps the sword in balance. Without the wisdom of the cup, the sword forgets who it's truly serving. Its strength and power without the wisdom of the cup becomes a destructive force.

And the cauldron, without the strength and integrity of the sword becomes not wisdom, but manipulation.

Chapter 7

To the Feet of the
Black Madonna

Peering through the shadows, our eyes meet. Hers are fierce yet reveal a humorous twinkle that only comes from journeying into the underworld and back again, a fearless gaze that knows the true comedy of life. I'm nervous, like a little child exploring a dark room that holds a secret I may not want to discover and knowing if I find it, my world will never be the same. I move closer, conscious of each small step not knowing if she is going to embrace me or annihilate me, an odd mixture of fear and desire. Her black form moves with the shadows, as though dancing with the unseen. This is the presence of the dark mother.

The only flights that Helena and I can get together arrive in France a couple days before the rest of the group. I'm thrilled to have this time alone with her, and when she tells me she's going to take me to somewhere special, climbing on my belly in a cold, dark cave isn't what I have in mind.

"I can't see ANYTHING!"

Panicked, I crawl through the dark cave, arms outstretched, searching for the walls and finding only black. Only cold, empty space.

"There are more ways to see than with your eyes," Helena replies calmly. "You've relied too much on light. Use your inner vision and sense where the opening is."

I don't know what Helena means by seeing in other ways. Frustration and fear take hold.

I can't do this!

My eyes start to well with tears as the darkness swallows me into its depths. A silent internal scream shatters what little sense of control remains.

Nothing is working for me in my life. Everything I wanted has fallen apart. I don't even know what I'm doing in this fucking cave!

An image of my ex-husband's face comes into view. A look of contempt as he sits behind his enormous mahogany desk, on his throne. A sneer followed by a pompous chuckle.

Hate.

I shudder, recoil and close my eyes. Again, the image preys upon me like a wild animal that's been lurking in the shadows.

"He wants your feminine power for himself," a voice in my head calmly states.

I remember him telling me once how he felt a woman should dress.

"That's not what being a woman is all about!" I screamed aloud, my face heated with rage. The memory is enough to re-fuel my fury.

My self-pity turns to sheer determination. With new-found inner strength, I pull myself out of the clutches of darkness. I refuse to live my life feeling powerless. Taking several deep breaths quiets the incessant, self-defeating chatter in my mind. I reach for the amulet of a snake that hangs around my neck and feel a calm and assured presence deep inside me.

The Goddess' ally.

I sense the opening I am looking for is to my right. With one arm outstretched, and a renewed sense of confidence, I continue crawling. Jagged rocks further bruise my tender knees and the open wounds on my hands sting. I find the cold, damp wall of the cave. I run my hand across its rough surface and feel a small opening near the bottom of the wall.

"I think I found it!" I announce, excitedly. "But it feels really narrow. Is there another opening?" I ask Helena, desperately hoping she isn't expecting me to fit through this tiny space.

"No, there's only one. You can slide through," she says convincingly, suddenly right behind me.

I was never one for tiny spaces, nor for heights, but I had made it this far back into the cave, and I know Helena won't let me retreat. I reach through the opening trying to get a sense of its depth. It feels significant, a thick wall of rock. Laying as flat as possible, with my arms, I drag my body over small, sharp stones. Eventually, my elbows no longer scrape along the sides of rock, and I slowly sit up, crouching down, unaware as to how large of a space I am in. Helena joins me, what seems to be a quick and graceful passage for her since the only groaning I heard was my own.

I spread my overly-worn sweatshirt onto the cool, dirt floor and make myself as comfortable as possible. I hear the strike of a match and am at once relieved by the soft glow of a single candle giving just enough light for me to see Helena's face.

Her penetrating gaze pierces the illusory walls of my persona. I feel uneasy, unsure of what is going to happen next. Her face shape-shifts within the light and shadows of the flickering candle. One minute she is old with etched lines and the next, a much younger woman tossing her dark auburn hair to the side.

She looks more like an owl than she usually does in this light.

We sit in silence, listening to the walls of the ancient cave, waiting for their whispers. Suddenly, Helena breaks the stillness.

"Power is cultivated from the inside," she says with her strong German accent. Her words are jolting, spoken with such conviction. I sit up taller, eagerly anticipating what she is going to say next.

"These people who wave their money around and puff up their chests as though they are better than others do not know what true power is," she says while waving her bony, talon-like finger.

"You, Treeesta, are on the path to finding true power." Helena's words land heavy in my chest. Fear clutches me and chills run up my spine. For a brief moment I want to run, but I force myself to breathe through it. It does no good to listen to fear. It never leads me to where I want to go.

I pull my sweatshirt out from under me and put it on. It's soft from years of use, and smells of wood smoke. I bury my head in its hood and hug my knees close to my chest, seeking comfort.

"Not to worry, the Dark Mother is with you." She smiles, her eyes softening.

Dark Mother? I can't find words to ask her what she means by dark.

"The dark is not to be feared. Yes, there are energies that we refer to as dark because they are undesirable. But there is also the dark realm of the mother that is life giving. It's like the fertile soil of the earth," she says as she scoops up a handful of dirt from the floor of the cave. "She is the grail," Helena says, letting the dry, loose soil slip between her fingers.

"It's the womb that is void of light that nourishes the fetus. Your knowing of this will come after you are initiated into the earth mysteries."

Though I don't yet understand what she's referring to, her words stir something deep in my own womb. I feel their truth.

I wake early from a restless night's sleep. Continual dreams of being back in the cave, sometimes with Helena, other times, my snake amulet shape shifts and slowly comes alive as it begins to slither up and around my neck. I give my body a good shake and take a hot shower to wash away both dirt and my disturbing dreams.

The rest of the group is arriving later in the day, so I head out on my own to stroll through the quaint French village.

Springtime in France is a very similar climate to Upstate NY. A chill is in the air, but the beautiful wisteria flowers are just coming into bloom. Where I live, I can't get wisteria to bloom. As hard as I try, it's just too cold. I stop for coffee and a croissant at a little cafe and sit outdoors watching the busy townspeople pass by. There are children dressed in uniform carrying their backpacks on their way to school, store owners opening up their shops, and a number of artists setting up their displays getting ready for the town's daily market. A couple walks by, arm in arm. The man bends down, takes the slender woman's face in his hands, and gives her a long, passionate kiss before crossing the busy street. I feel a pang of longing as I watch them, then turn away.

I turn my attention to the warmth of the morning sun shining down on my face, and I admire the vines that have found their way up the sides of stone buildings, creating a canopy of pale, purple flowers draped over the doorways. Enjoying my buttery, flaky croissant, I listen to the chatter of French people and try to understand at least one or two words. My years of French classes in high school and college give me enough of a familiarity of the language, but in the moment, I feel pretty inept.

Tired and bruised from the previous day's experience, I close my eyes soaking in all the sounds of car horns and people talking and the smell of fresh bread and strong coffee wafting from the countless cafes. I turn my palms upward and let the warm sun heal small gashes that still sting — remnants from the cave's jagged walls. Here I am, in France, a country known for both romance and mystery, and despite my tiredness, I keep thinking of the man I met over the phone, just two weeks before leaving.

A couple weeks back, I had a dream. I'm on a fancy boat, more like a cruise ship, dressed all in white. I'm with a man, who's also dressed in white. He appears to be of Spanish descent, dark hair, tan skin. He looks like Julio Iglesias, the singer from the 80's. I hear the message, "This is a sacred marriage." I wake feeling intoxicated with love. I lie in bed not wanting to abandon the feeling, surrendering and letting it infuse me, but I'm clear I do not want to meet a man. I have no interest in having a relationship. I figure the dream is more about my inner relationship with my masculine self. I've been divorced almost three years and honestly, I don't want to be bothered with a relationship. So, I dismiss it.

Just a couple of days later, the kids and I pick up our monthly food order from the co-op and are carrying the boxes into the house. Matthew goes over to the blinking answering machine and hits the play button. I hear a man's voice saying that he's received my letter and would be happy to talk with me. I don't think much of it until he says his name is Ricardo Sierra. I nearly drop the box of food I'm carrying. Hearing the Spanish name after having the dream only a couple of days previously leaves me frozen in my tracks. It rattles me to my core. I know this is no coincidence, and I put off returning his call for days.

The letter is one of 25 that Kelly and I sent to people who are creating nature-based communities. We hope to reach other like-minded colleagues. The only person we hear back from is Ricardo who runs a summer camp called, Hawk Circle.

"Why don't you want to call him back?" Kelly pries.

"I'm too scared," I respond half chuckling and half serious.

"Why?" Kelly asks with a twinkle in her eye.

"Because…it feels like a big deal. It feels like it's going to lead to something that I'm just not ready for. And my dream…well, yeah, I'm just not ready. I don't want a relationship," I answer quite emphatically. I'm just not ready to accept my fate. That's what it feels like. My future showing up on my doorstep and me doing everything I can to hold the door shut.

Since my divorce, I am finally creating my life the way I want. The kids and I have a nice home out in the country, right across the road from my parents, and I'm excited for the direction my life is taking. Adding another person is just going to create confusion.

As I'm getting into my car one day, I notice two hawks flying over my house. *No biggie, that's not an unusual thing to see living out in the country.* When I return home, there are still two hawks circling overhead. I still shrug it off. The hawks are there the next morning, and the sight of them makes me really dig my heels in as if they're solely responsible for pushing me to do something I don't want to do.

The next day, I'm driving home from the grocery store and a hawk swoops down from a tree and heads right towards my windshield. I slam on the breaks as it glides over the top of my car just missing getting hit.

"Okay, okay, okay!" I shout, banging my hands against the steering wheel.

Because Ricardo's business is named Hawk Circle, I can no longer ignore the message from the hawks.

I call him that night. He wants to meet, but I'm heading for France in just a few days. We talk over the phone until the middle of the night, not about anything too personal, more about our work. I'm so comfortable talking with him as though I've known him all my life. We keep it more of a business call than anything else, but now and then I find myself imagining getting to know him more. We set up a time to meet when I return from France. His voice is like a musical note when played just right, like a song you want to listen to over and over again.

Now here I am, sitting in a little French village, daydreaming of a man I've never met. There's something about meeting someone over the phone before meeting them in person that allows you to really connect with their essence. He reminds me of the masculine energy I felt from the standing stone at the Ring of Brodgar in Scotland.

I wonder if my experience with the stone actually set this whole meeting in motion. I remember the passion and the familiarity that I felt when I was leaning up against the stone. I imagine it as a portal that activated an internal compass, helping me to find him.

Life often takes us in unexpected directions. Imagining being with him floods my thoughts. I try to shove them away and make excuses, but I can't deny the tug of attraction. Does my soul recognize him as someone I once knew and loved? Or maybe it's the amorous atmosphere of France that gives me a different perspective, but whoever Ricardo Sierra is, I'm falling in love with him.

Waking from my daydream, I glance at my watch and notice I have only two hours left before the rest of our group shows up. Swinging my backpack over my shoulder, I pull out my newly exchanged Euros, and proudly say to the waitress, "Combien?" When she understands me, I'm thrilled and pay the bill. Then I set off to explore as much as I can before meeting up with the rest of the group and heading to Chartres.

A couple hours later, I join the group and climb the steps to board the bus. I hear a familiar voice and look up. Sitting in the driver's seat is Harry, our driver from our trip to the British Isles.

"Well, well, fancy meeting you again!" Harry says grinning from ear to ear. Despite his unsettling experience at the Brodgar stone circle, Harry later shares with us that his tour with us changed his life, and he had hurried home to tell his wife all about his experience. Wanting to support Helena's work, he offered to drive our group through France.

"Harry! So good to see you. What a pleasant surprise," I said giving him a big hug before finding a seat.

The town of Chartres is only about an hour away and home to the most magnificent cathedral I've ever seen. I remember reading one of Joseph Campbell's books saying he visited Chartres every year to sit in the cathedral and contemplate his life and his work. I completely understand his reasoning the moment I set foot in Chartres.

The rest of the group and I stand in front of the main entrance of the cathedral, huddling close to Helena as she talks about its history. "The Templars were master builders. They started building in 1194 and it took them 26 years to complete," says Helena, leaning in closer. "They knew they were building on sacred ground, so they built the whole cathedral working in complete silence." Helena shares with us quietly as other visitors pass by.

I stare up at the grand structure. I had seen its twin spires from miles away before reaching the small town of Chartres. They're a beacon of light exuding a formidable power. The intricate details of carvings on the stone facade is awe inspiring, and reveal its connection to mystery traditions, despite being a catholic church. Its majestic presence is humbling.

As I walk through the main entrance with heavy, carved wooden doors, I see the famous labyrinth. A hushed silence blankets the cathedral—a silence of reverence and awe. I pause, taking in the beauty and notice the soft colors of reds and blues and greens that emanate from the rose window up above.

Following in the footsteps of pilgrimages seeking to become closer to God or to ask for repentance, our group slowly and deliberately traverses the stone pathway of the labyrinth. Spending time walking back and forth within each of the four quadrants, my mind wanders to the four directions, the four elements, the four seasons, the four suits of a tarot deck.

As we complete our walk, we disperse to corners of the cathedral for our own time of praying. I head to the back and find the statue of the Black Madonna, all decorated with shimmering, gold fabric, a vivid contrast to her dark-toned face. She looks so regal, perched high on her throne. Candles are lit all around her and old, French women dressed in dark and unobtrusive clothes, wearing white lace scarves over their heads, are kneeling at the wooden pews, praying.

I imagine the petite, stout, French women waiting for their husbands to leave for work, tidying up the house, hanging up their aprons, and checking themselves in the mirror while carefully covering their heads with their delicate, lace scarves. Then with purse in hand, setting off down the winding, cobblestone streets, waving to long-time friends and store merchants as they make their daily visit to the Black Madonna.

This is so different from what I experienced growing up. Sundays were more of a ritual of dressing up in our best clothes to sit for a one-hour service — a dutiful obligation. We bowed our heads and prayed when told and sang the most god-awful songs. All the while the true source of God was just outside the window. The sun shone through the stained glass windows and the tree branches danced in the wind as if the Divine was saying, "Here I am. I'm right here."

I observe the women, with such apparent devotion and love for her. And by the looks of their furrowed brows and closed eyes, they are really praying. Not the kind of praying that becomes a habitual stream of words spoken as your mind wanders in a million different directions. Real prayer, focused prayer. Prayers that you need answered.

At this point in my life, I know nothing of the Black Madonna. I've been raised Protestant and the feminine principle of the Protestant religion is non-existent.

I remember when I was little, probably about 11 years old, sitting in church with my family. I didn't usually listen to much the minister was talking about. It was boring and I spent most of my time drawing on the Sunday program. But one day, I heard him mention Mary Magdalene, referring to her as the "whore that Jesus saved." In that moment, something inside of me woke up, momentarily, like a sleeping lion that suddenly leaps to the sounds of a possible threat. I was jolted out of my own world of drawing and doodling and felt rage rise up, and the words inside my head silently shouting, "SHE WAS NOT A WHORE!"

I was thankful the words didn't come blaring out of my mouth. It would have caused quite the stir amongst the congregation that seemed to sit there half listening, half dozing. And I wouldn't have been able to explain myself at all, because even I didn't understand where the words came from. Looking back, I see that my goddess self, my divine feminine self, has been with me all along, just not really awakened, raising her head and voice in brief moments as this.

"I'd like to meet you, to know more about you. I pray that will happen on this journey," I say, kneeling in a wooden pew in the far back of the cathedral. I rise and walk down to the front, light a candle and place it near her statue, before joining the rest of the group.

The next day we head to Vezelay, where there's a beautiful cathedral dedicated to Mary Magdalene. I fall in love with this town the moment I see it. It's pretty much a one-street town lined with restaurants, art galleries, a few gift shops and cafes that leads to the very top of the hill, to the perfectly poised cathedral.

We have the day to explore, so I follow the cobblestone street that leads to the cathedral overlooking the small village. It's an immense structure denoting the sacredness and reverence for Mary Magdalene. As I walk through the double-doored entryway, divided by an elaborately carved stone pillar, my breath quickens as I sit in the nearest pew. Its awesomeness takes some time for me to absorb. A small chorus is singing, their voices like angels, fill the cathedral with an extraordinary vibration of light. Leaving my seat, I slowly walk down the outer side of the rows of countless, wooden pews, searching for the entryway to the basilica of Mary Magdalene. Finding an old, stone staircase, I descend, the angelic voices growing more and more obscure and the air noticeably cooler. The small enclave is dimly lit except for her relics that are displayed in a glass case. I sit down in one of the simple wooden chairs that are placed in front of the window of her relics, remembering my eleven-year-old self's first encounter with her in church.

"You've been so misunderstood," I say repeatedly. While I speak these words to the relics of Mary Magdalene, I'm aware that I'm also saying them to myself. I feel the pain of being misunderstood, rejected and banished. I hold no memories in this lifetime of being banished, but somewhere deep inside, the church's rejection of her is also the rejection of me as a woman. It feels like a knife piercing my heart as I get a momentary glimpse into the church's burial chambers.

Hearing the ringing of the church's bells, I leave to meet everyone at a little restaurant down the street. The restaurant is a cozy, old stone house with slanted floors and hand-hewn timbers. Our group, tired from our day of travel, finds a table in the back and settles in. We are a diverse group of women, some older and a few about my age. We stuff ourselves on cheeses and breads and fresh, roasted vegetables and chicken slathered in butter and garlic. The waiter serves us wine in a hand-thrown pottery pitcher. As I pour the deep, red wine into my glass, I think of Mary Magdalene as the carrier of the grail. The pitcher has a real earthy and primitive look to it and yet holds this elegant wine, red like blood. Seeing a stack of other like pitchers, I ask our waiter if I can buy one. I leave with a beautiful, greenish-brown speckled pitcher, sticky with red wine dripping down its sides. I am touching on the very edges of the grail and the Magdalene consciousness.

As we make our way deeper into the mysteries of the Black Madonna, and into the South of France, I become more and more curious. She obviously is powerful, I can feel that, but I still don't quite understand her. She's so revered by the French people as is Mary Magdalene, and I so badly want to understand it all. But some things are meant to be experienced to be really understood. The layer of Christian beliefs that molded and shaped me up to this point is dropping away like an old, worn-out robe as deeper truths are revealed.

We enter into Cathar country where the teachings of Mary Magdalene and the Essenes have been preserved for many years by the Cathars. They, as Helena describes them, were called "the good people." A kind and generous group that quietly practiced their own beliefs, honoring the feminine and the teachings that Mary Magdalene brought to the south of France years earlier. This area of France is a wilderness with winding roads that lead us through small towns tucked in and around the tree-covered mountains.

As we come to Montsegur, one of the ruins of a Cathar castle that sits high on top of a mountain, I feel more and more agitated. At this time in my life, I didn't always take a moment to ask myself why I might be feeling this way, nor did I have the understanding of how the land holds consciousness of past events. But now, having gotten off the bus and standing at the foot of Montsegur, seeing its remains resting at the very top of the mountain, I feel completely unhinged.

"Helena! I'm feeling really out of sorts, like I want to run and scream," I tell her as I run and catch up with her.

"Here, take some of this. It will help. This is old inquisition stuff. Just let it go," she says as she gives me her bottle of flower essence and then turns to address the group.

"This is where the Cathars were killed. Montsegur was their last stronghold before the Romans and the Royal Catholic French troops killed them, most being burned alive at the stake." Our group huddles closer to listen to Helena describe the horrific fate of the Cathars. It's apparent from her voice and fierce look in her eyes that she's not just sharing historical facts, this is personal. In fact, it's always personal to Helena. I'd hear the disgust, sometimes sorrow, other times fury in her voice.

"Take a few drops of the flower essence that Trista has. It will help any of you who are picking up on what happened. It gets stuck in the land, these events. As we heal our own memories and offer our prayers, the land heals, too," she says. The flower essence calms my nerves, and we continue up the path to explore the ancient ruins.

The ruins sit atop a mountain with a steep climb being its only access. They look over a valley and a small village below. This magnificent view feels so familiar to me. I easily imagine myself as a Cathar. Living peacefully, high atop the mountain. Making my way down to the small village below where animals grazed and people tended their flocks of sheep. Up here, I feel the peace of the Cathar people, but below, quite the opposite.

Later, we continue our way to a nearby town, where we stop in the square for lunch at an outdoor cafe. I go into the public restroom. I'm in one of the stalls when I hear the door to the bathroom squeak open and someone walk in. Without hesitation, I leap up onto the toilet seat so no one can see my feet and know I'm in here. I'm perched on top of the toilet — a response so instinctual that my mind is trying to catch up.

What the hell am I doing?

I leap off the seat as quickly as I had leaped on, and shake my arms and legs, trying to rid myself of the need to hide.

I wonder how many people went into hiding during the inquisition right in this area. Someone might have been hiding in this very same spot, afraid for their life as the soldiers hunted them down. Am I just picking up on what's happened here or am I remembering a past life where I was the one being hunted?

I go back to our table at the cafe and share my experience with the group.

"The human body is a powerful instrument. Our bodies can feel what's being held in the earth and through our bodies we can help heal these events both for ourselves and for the earth," says Helena.

"What's the best way to work through it?" asks Jenny, a middle-aged woman from Ohio.

"Well..." Helena carefully answers, "I feel it is about the relationship we have between our own bodies and the earth. Allowing ourselves to feel deeply what is coming up for us and then do whatever you have to, cry, yell, scream, punch a pillow. Whatever it takes to let go cleanses both our bodies and the earth."

"We've been so domesticated, as women..." I chime in.

"Absolutely! We've been so trained as women to be nice and kind and polite — all the bullshit that keeps us in line," Helena agrees, passionately.

"It's the Black Madonna, the fiery, force of transformation that helps to unleash our power," she says. "Otherwise, it gets buried deep in our wombs, which is not good," continues Helena.

I love listening to Helena talk. She's so ardent when she's teaching.

Our next stop is at a small, modest cathedral that sits by itself at the end of a country road lined with large oak trees. The trees had been planted intentionally as a resource for wood when the church needed restoration perhaps a couple hundred years in the future. By then the trees would have grown to just the right size to mill into strong and sturdy beams, replacing any inside the church that had weakened over time. *Incredibly wise planning.*

Before going inside the church, Helena leads us into a garden, still covered with its winter layer of mulch. In the back of the garden, stands a six foot white statue of Mother Mary. I listen to Helena describe a ley line that connects this statue with the Black Madonna statue inside the church, a line of energy in the earth that both statues anchor.

Our group follows Helena inside the small stone cathedral to the back where the Black Madonna statue stands. We settle into the folding chairs that are lined in rows, taking time to gather our own thoughts and to pray. One by one, we make our way up to stand in front of Her. Helena stands nearby. When it's my turn, I slowly approach her. She's wearing an ivory, satin robe and is encased in a gold rimmed, glass case. Aside from my visit to Chartres, I've never stood in front of a statue asking for guidance or a blessing. My Protestant religion is void of revering any statue or saint, but I stand there anyways. Having observed the French women's reverence for the Black Madonna, I trust she has something to teach me. A few minutes pass, I turn to go back to my seat, but Helena quickly puts her hand on my back, stopping me.

"Look into her eyes," she says. I look at her confused, wondering why she's holding me there. I turn back to stare into the Madonna's eyes that seem to be laughing as she's looking slightly off to the side.

What is Helena wanting me to see?

Continuing to search the eyes of the Black Madonna, I ask, "What do you have to show me?" A few awkward moments pass with Helena standing right next to me, while I stare at the statue, other members of our group waiting patiently.

I'm just about to give up, when I feel an energy pierce my heart like someone shooting an arrow of light into my chest, shattering it open into a million pieces.

Her message, very clearly transferred is, "Don't be afraid to love again."

Tears trickle down my face and my heart opens, like a spacious cavern. I didn't realize that my heart was even closed, especially after "meeting" Ricardo over the phone before leaving for France, so assume it has to do with my divorce. But I soon realize, this isn't about healing my broken heart. This is a healing of my soul's heart, my divine feminine self that's preparing to emerge, to awaken, to come out of the dark cave of my inner most sanctuary where she's been hiding for, I don't know, maybe a couple thousand years?

Helena gives me a big hug and whispers in my ear, "She wants you to have one of her flowers." Holding my hand, she pulls me over to a large, flowering violet plant where I pick a deep purple flower. I hold it to my heart feeling so blessed, but not really knowing the extent of what just happened.

I follow Helena over to a small, interesting statue of Mary Magdalene. The statue reveals her age that's more true to reality than the images of a young, beautiful, long-haired woman that we most often see.

"Pay attention to the positioning of her hands," Helena whispers.

I notice she holds her hands in the typical fashion of *as above, so below,* however, I also notice her hand positioning is reversed with her left hand pointing up instead of down. This is just one of many subtle messages the artists and sculptors from long ago leave for us future seekers of truth. A trail of symbols and clues that reveal a more accurate history of Christianity. I can feel that Mary Magdalene is revealing a deeper truth hidden beneath layers of wrongful myths and stories.

"Is she trying to tell us that the truth is the reverse of what we've been told?" I ask Helena.

"Hmmm, I believe so Treeesta. Interesting, right?" says Helena.

We continue our journey through Cathar country to our next destination, Rennes le Chateau. I read a book on Helena's recommended reading list, *Holy Blood, Holy Grail* by Michael Baigent, Richard Leigh, and Henry Lincoln. The authors go into great detail about the mysterious happenings at Rennes le Chateau with the abbe Berenger Sauniere and the treasure supposedly found on its premises. According to their findings, it is believed that what had remained hidden here at this small cathedral in the mountains of southern France contained information that would rewrite Christianity's religious history.

I'm excited to visit this place so steeped in mystery. As we drive up the narrow road to the small, hillside village, I see a cluster of old stone houses and the Magdalene tower perched at the top of the hill. An older woman rushes out to meet us, frantically waving her arms at our bus to stop. The little village is pretty much deserted except for her. She's the caretaker that lives near the small church and tends to its upkeep.

"Stop! Stop!" She yells as she rushes towards us.

"You cannot visit here today," she says in her broken English, panting.

"Why not?" Helena asks, brow furrowed as she stands on the steps to our bus.

"Last night someone came and broke into the cathedral and beheaded Asmodeus," she says with apparent sadness and despair.

Asmodeus is the demon statue that guards the entryway to the small cathedral.

"They slashed my tires, too! It's not safe for you to be here," she adds.

What the hell? What time period have I just entered?

This situation seems so archaic to me. It wakes me up to the reality of how desperate some people are to maintain the church's teachings. Now I'm even more interested than before regarding the mysteries of Rennes le Chateau.

Helena hugs the poor woman goodbye and returns to the bus. We are all shocked and saddened.

"These people are *crazy!*" says Helena throwing her arms up in the air.

"Can you imagine someone coming here and beheading the statue? They'll stop at nothing to hide the truth! And the poor woman who looks after the cathedral...," she shakes her head in dismay.

I'm disappointed we can't visit Rennes le Chateau and find it hard to believe that this type of ill-intended act of vandalism is still going on. I'm shocked by the extreme measures that people are taking to keep the teachings of Mary Magdalene hidden — teachings I'm just beginning to understand. I'm inspired now more than ever to dive deep into her teachings to find out what others are so intent on suppressing. But as Helena has told me many times, I'm not going to find what I'm looking for in a book. This is going to be a deep dive into my sacred womb, my own grail and Divine feminine. This is the only way for me to truly understand her.

Traveling deeper into Southern France, from Cathar country to Provence coincides with traveling deeper into my femininity. We stay in the quiet, little seaside town of Saints Maries de la Mer, right on the shore of the Mediterranean. The beautiful little town, where legends say Mary Magdalene landed after fleeing from Jerusalem, pregnant with her daughter, is brimming with the Romani people. They're setting up their tents in preparation for the annual *Festival of St. Sarah* which is only days away. Thousands of people will be gathering and parading down the streets, carrying the beautiful Saint Sarah statue, patron saint to the Romani. She'll be elegantly adorned with lace and satin and carried to the shores of the sea before being returned to her crypt. We are told the whole event has a primal atmosphere with days of music, drinking and flamenco dancing in the streets. Unfortunately, by the time the festivities start, we'll already be back in Paris.

As I stroll through the charming town, I wander into their market. Bright, colorful garments hang from their tents, white peasant-style tops, hand-embroidered with colorful threads and full-flowing skirts of every color imaginable. The Roma come primarily from the rural areas of France and Catalonia often speaking their own unique dialect. Most have dark, weathered faces with long, unkept hair that hang wildly past their shoulders. They appear to wear all the clothes they own at once with layers of bright colorful skirts and blouses and old, worn out shoes. The smells of pungent herbs hanging in bunches from the ceilings of their tents and burning incense of patchouli waft through the market. Their eyes remind me of a feral cat, alive and untamable. It all stirs my own longing for a creative, primal life.

I felt detached and dispassionate before coming on this trip. I remember when I visited Kelly at her house one day as she was baking. I sat and watched her sifting the flour and sprinkling in spices and pouring a cup of melted butter into the bowl. As I watched her stir the ingredients together, I felt something stir inside of me. I missed this feeling of passion in my life. It was an alchemical moment. And now, I'm feeling my passion stir awake.

Growing up, my family was pretty conservative. Experiencing pleasure in my body or expressing my emotions, whether sadness, anger or joy wasn't part of the experience. My parents were loving and nurturing, but in a white bread sort of way. My mother didn't ever cook with spices and herbs, and I grew up craving a more savory life. I think this is what compelled me to teach myself to bake and to cook when I was 14 years old. I was hungry for a different way of life. I craved deep feeling and passionate living. The Black Madonna herself. Fresh vegetables, aromatic herbs from Provence, spices from the Middle East, dark chocolate, nakedness and curvy hips is what I longed for then, but with little understanding. A delectable sensuality. And now, years later, it's the very path I'm pursuing.

The past few years, being a single mom has taken its toll. Being both mother and father to my children leaves little time for me to step out of the role of the responsible parent. My maiden self craves expression, connection and love making. My thoughts return to Ricardo. I inhale his essence that I had a glimpse of during our phone call and rouse my sensual self.

As I stand on the shores of the cool, sparkling waters of the Mediterranean, saying goodbye, my body softens with each gentle wave upon the sandy beach. I feel relief from holding things together, maintaining a sense of strength and perseverance that has helped me to make the changes in my life. The hardness ebbs away and a warm, juicy flow of passion begins to forge new pathways in my life.

Our trip is coming to an end. Our last night is spent in an elegant, stone villa where we share a delicious meal of Chicken Basquaise and Bouride, a fish stew laden with aioli sauce and our last creme brûlée.

"Here's to an amazing journey with you beautiful women! The Black Madonna has carried us well. May she be with you when you return to your homes where she'll inevitably work her magic into your lives!" Helena says as she raises her glass of wine. We all raise our glasses and there are tears, and hoots and hollers and so much love shared before we sleepily, head off for bed.

I catch my reflection in a nearby mirror, and it stops me in my tracks. I take a second look. I'm dressed all in white wearing an elegant wedding gown. Am I getting married? I see before me the entry way to the cathedral and the turned heads with the eyes of a hundred guests eagerly anticipating my arrival with what appears to be my own wedding.

At the far end of the church, I see my groom, my husband to be, dressed in his royal regale, all befitting of a king. Waistcoat adorned with shiny, gold buttons, white pants, shiny, black leather boots and a bejeweled crown upon his head.

I begin to take slow, hesitant steps down the red carpeted aisle while all the time holding the gaze of my King. His eyes are a pool of blue and green that hold the gateway to my future. But rather than feeling love and joy, I see the shackles of responsibility that come with taking my place next to him. Faces of pompous royalty flash before my eyes with a constant flow of obligatory wifely duties, my queen's forced smile adhered to my face. A life of societal expectations and propriety, a continual masquerade unfolds as I make my way down the aisle.

The shackles tighten, my breath dwindles as I near the end of the red carpet. With my eyes still fixed upon the loving gaze of my king, I hear a door creak and without turning, can feel a familiar presence standing in the back of the cathedral.

My heart beats faster, and I slowly turn. Dressed in a pair of black jeans and a slightly worn black t-shirt, I see him — it's the magician. His dark brown eyes mirror to me a different life. His presence alone ignites something deep inside me, a fire that wants to burn hot with an untamable wildness. He reaches his hand out, with pleading eyes, to rescue me from a fate that would surely leave me emaciated of spirit.

The conflict in this moment is like an ice pick gouging at my heart. The eyes of a hundred guests, once joyful change to a palette of question, disgust, and for some rage as they see me wavering. Do I obey the expectations of the King and the people? Do I abandon the wild part of me that is stirred to life by the magician's outreached hand? Do I give myself over for the wants of others?

I am torn, not wanting to hurt my King, abandon him at the altar. Nor do I want to subscribe to the forsaken landscape of my soul. But I know if I continue down the red-carpeted aisle, the mounting rage and fear of the guests will return to a place of joy and pleasantness and order. It is all in my hands.

I turn once again, meeting the dark pool of the magician's eyes, and he beckons me with an undeniable truth. "You are more than this. Don't give in. Don't surrender your power to a life of expectations. The safety of this life is all but an illusion."

I quickly turn to meet the gaze of my King, mouthing the words, "I'm sorry" as I turn away and begin to sprint, catching the hand of the magician as we leap into the air and take off flying, my beautiful gown falling below onto the raging and appalled guests. I am free.

As soon as I realize I'm flying, I plummet through the air with what feels like a hard landing back in my body, and I'm startled awake. I lay in bed, catching my breath, taking notice of all the details of this incredibly symbolic dream. I smile to myself. I'm letting go of the life of a queen marrying the king where no doubt there would be further domestication, dutifulness, and a cultivated life. I'm choosing the magician, a life of mystical pursuit, uncovering my wildness, seeking freedom and unearthing life's hidden mysteries.

After showering and packing my belongings, I bound down the stairs and join the others for our final breakfast together. Helena comes into the room all a flurry as she often does. I've actually never seen her saunter into a room. Her petite body comes with a large aura that acts as a gust of wind that would send a table full of papers flying. She's especially this way this morning as she's handling all the details of our final day and making sure we're at the airport in time for our return flights.

Our eyes meet, and I give her a smile. She comes over and standing behind me grabs my shoulders, bends down and says, "Well, well, well, what did you do last night?"

"I went flying," I whisper to her. "I'll tell you all about it on the flight home."

She lets out a hearty belly laugh and scurries off to tend to her business.

As I leave the mystical land of France, my thoughts return to home, the kids, and to Ricardo. My heart feels so open, my body so alive. While I have yet to fully understand the powers of the Black Madonna and Mary Magdalene, I feel awake in my body more than I ever have.

"Goodbye beautiful France! I'll be back."

Chapter 8
Gateway to Passion

Your warm breath on my neck sends shivers up my spine. Every cell in my body awakening and responding to your gentle touch like a bud opening to the warm rays of the summer sun. My lips meet yours, and I inhale your essence that fuels my passion and opens my garden gate. Enter beloved and I will douse you with my own sweet honey that flows from between my legs.

Walking through the woods, Ricardo studies the trees we pass that are just leafing out. He stops momentarily to observe the antics of a raven sitting on a branch overhead, tracking everything around him as relentlessly as I track everything inside of me. He has a reverence for nature and all things wild. His dark eyes are like a hawk's, noting an animal's footprint, tracking it through the soft spring ground onto the damp leaves of the forest floor. I study him like a fox sitting at the edge of a field, wondering if it's safe to come out in the open.

A few days after returning home from France, I called him, feeling pretty nervous. *Was I the only one that is experiencing an attraction?* Maybe I've made the whole thing up prior to my trip to France. After all, we've only talked on the phone once. But as soon as I hear his voice, I feel the familiar ache inside and the desire to know him more. We talk late into the night, and after several more phone conversations that follow over the next couple of weeks, we plan our first meeting.

It was the next natural step, but I felt a lot of resistance to meeting in person. Everything had moved so quickly since my return home. I clung to the life that was familiar, the comfort of just the three of us, Matthew, Jessi and me. I loved the three of us. It worked. But I couldn't ignore what was opening up for me. It was like kayaking on a river where you get swept up into the strong current and you have no choice but to flow with it.

As the day to meet neared, my resistance was a growing concern.

Should I cancel? Should I just let go of all of this and pretend it never happened?

I took the children to the park at the end of the lake. It was still springtime, so it wasn't officially open, and I knew we'd most likely be the only ones there. I brought a picnic lunch and a bottle of water from Lourdes that one of our group members brought back from her solo journey to the healing waters. I needed help with letting go. I had been increasingly agitated as though I was being torn in two, part of me wanting to see what this new direction was all about, and the other part wanting to stay put.

When we got to the park, dark clouds were rolling in, but we still had time to play in the sand before any rain let loose. We ran around on the cold, wet beach in our bare feet, threw sticks out into the water for Bradford to chase and then ran for cover under the pavilion just before the rain poured down. Bolts of lightning crackled from the sky followed by deep roars of thunder. Powerful gusts of wind bent the old willow tree that stood at the edge of the lake until its branches were touching the ground. It was an awesome, wild storm!

This was exactly what I needed to clear my uncertainty and my threads of resistance that clung to the past. I grabbed the bottle of water from Lourdes and ran out into the storm and poured the healing water over my head as the rain tumbled down, flattening my hair to my face. The wind surged around me tearing away my attachments I had to my old life. The kids screamed and laughed wondering what the heck I was doing as I ran back to the pavilion for safe cover.

I was cleansed of how I thought my life should look like. My beliefs were stripped away, and I was completely open as I gave myself over to whatever was to come. Like a continuation of my dream in France. I was choosing a less than conventional life and for that matter, a man who did not live by societal expectations.

So now, here I am, walking through the woods with him, so familiar to me in many ways, yet still a complete stranger. I imagine us having been together for countless lifetimes, playing different roles, knowing that we'd meet again and again and again.

"Look for me in the wilderness," I imagine him saying to me before we were both born into this lifetime.

He runs a wilderness camp for kids. His dark, thick hair smells of campfire smoke, and his hands are strong and rough from making hand-drill fires and throwing wooden spears. He's passionate about connecting children to nature. His eyes light up every time he shares stories about his summer camp.

We spend the spring and summer getting to know one another, talking on the phone as often as possible. Since we live two hours away from one another, our visits aren't as frequent as we'd like, but they're weekends we both look forward to and count the days until we see one another again. My trip to the Black Madonna prepared me for this relationship journey in so many ways. Years of feeling emotionally unsafe with my husband and a traumatic birth with Jessi has taken its toll. And the three years following our divorce, my inner warrior took over and I focused only on making sure the kids had what they needed with little time for myself. But now, I'm deeply connected to my body and alive in a way I haven't felt since I was a teenager. I'm reclaiming my feminine power.

Our visits are an alchemical blending of desire, the earthy scent of the forests and the heat of the summer sun. We swim naked in the cool, woodland streams behind his house and make love in a nearby field beneath the silvery light of the moon. It's a feast of every imaginable food for the senses. An impeccable blend of pleasure and passion. There's something about his presence that gives me permission to open up to my pent up desires.

One evening, alone at home, I go to bed thinking about him, wishing he was lying next to me. I reach my hand down to pleasure myself, imagining his woodsy smell and gentle touch. When I climax, the warm river of the goddess flows down my thighs, and energy pulsates through my body like the swelling of ocean waves. *I had forgotten this.* I'm so grateful for the return, like a long lost lover. For years my orgasms felt forced, restricted and dry, the result of being the domesticated feminine. Now, the gateway to my sacred garden is open and it feels beautiful and life giving.

"Hand me the mortar and pestle," I ask Ricardo. We're making enchiladas for dinner during his weekend visit. From behind, he wraps his strong arms around me. Together, we grind the hot, chiltepin peppers, adding them to the red sauce cooking on the stove.

I feel almost shy. I was so alone in my previous marriage, assigned to the role of mother and housekeeper. We never shared intimate moments such as cooking together, nor was there any passion or desire for me as a woman. Now, I'm with Ricardo who is so willing to share every aspect of life.

Robbie Robertson's song, *Broken Arrow,* plays in the background. His words capture the moment so precisely. *Do you feel what I feel? Can we make it so it's part of the deal. I've gotta hold you in these arms of steel. Lay your heart on the line.*

Gently taking the pestle from my hand, Ricardo turns me to face him.

"Are you laying your heart on the line?" he asks.

"Yes," I mumble, my face flushing. I'm choosing to love again. Choosing to trust again and praying to God this isn't all a lie.

Reaching behind me, Ricardo turns off the stove. He slowly unbuttons my dress, while staring at me intently with his dark, brown eyes.

"Should we finish making dinner before we...?" I ask, my voice trailing off as Ricardo slides off my underwear and drops to his knees.

"Dinner can wait," he says, as his face disappears between my legs.

This journey with Ricardo is so freeing and empowering, but it isn't devoid of fear. The more I explore my power as a woman and the sensuousness of my body, the more aware I am of the messaging from my Christian background. It's like a piece of woven fabric when you begin to tug at the threads one at a time. The weave loosens and unravels until eventually, all you have is a pile of string. I have moments of ecstasy followed by jolts of fear at opening a forbidden door. And the threads I tug on are shame and judgment with harsh rights and wrongs.

I remember sitting next to my mom and playing with her hand. I was about seven years old.

"Doesn't this feel good, Mommy?" I ask as I very lightly touch my finger to the palm of her hand and draw a spiral.

"That's not something you should do," she says gently, but with apparent nervousness as she pulls her hand away.

I immediately retreated and felt my face become flush. There were several instances growing up that I reveled in the sensuousness of my body, but the message was clear. It wasn't appropriate or good to experience the delightful sensations that my body had to offer. As I grew into my teenage years, I felt even more shame as I experienced my sexuality and the sensations that were even more heightened than when I was younger. I guess this is where the term, *guilty pleasures,* comes from.

I begin to understand the path of Mary Magdalene and why she was banished so long ago. She's reminding me of the beautiful gift of my body and the power of my sexuality. I meet my wildness that's untamable, not easily controlled nor susceptible to succumbing to a life lived in fear. The goddess-self that lives by her own rules.

The more I free myself of restricting beliefs, the more the mystery of her teachings reveal themselves. Where once deprived, now I'm drinking in the vital elixir of the Goddess as I open to my sexual nature.

As a mother, this journey has its challenges. I have a wonderfully nurturing mother and grandmother, but never experience them as passionate and sexual women. I crave to see the two aspects of the feminine combined. I think about the feminine archetypes in my life. Mary, mother of Jesus, depicted as being loving and pure and unobtainable — the Virgin. And then the other Mary, Mary Magdalene, depicted as a whore. Such strong imprints on women over hundreds of years. No wonder we have such a hard time unearthing our powers.

I grew up believing that the acceptable role for a woman was to be a nurturing mother as pure as snow. To connect with your power as a sexual being was to risk public shame as a whore. Or worse, when the church went after so many female healers and priestesses, claiming them to be witches, tying their feet and hands to a pole in the town square, and publicly humiliating them before burning them at the stake. I remember this, somewhere in my DNA, I remember the smell of my own burning flesh. Sometimes I wake abruptly in the middle of the night with a gasp. I feel like a hunted animal. Panicked, frozen, fearing I'll be found.

Despite these fears, I refuse to let them paralyze me. My desire to experience passion and power outweigh my fear. And I feel incredibly safe with Ricardo. He hasn't been so influenced by the church and his family's beliefs as I have. His nonchalant attitude soothes my edges, and his desire to experience my passion gives me permission.

I hadn't realized I was hiding a part of myself until someone or a situation spoke to that part of me. When Ricardo and I were first getting to know one another over the phone, prior to meeting in person, he invited me to play along with envisioning us meeting for the first time. We both imagined meeting on a secluded beach. When he asked me what I would be wearing, I said a slinky black dress, but as soon as the words escaped, I felt fear that I was revealing too much, betraying the persona of the spiritual nice girl.

He responded, "Oh, I imagined you saying a long, floating white dress."

I immediately shrank back into hiding wishing I had never said anything, relieved that he couldn't see my face blushing with embarrassment. I said nothing. My Irish, youthful, round face and blond hair easily hides the dark-haired, passionate Latin woman that lives inside of me.

"I like that. You're like the unexpected librarian," he said, finally, relieving me of my moment of uncertainty. And so it began. Our passionate love affair.

The energy that is cultivated between us is like floating in the warm amniotic fluids of the primordial mother's birth waters combined with the fire of an active volcano. Eventually most of the threads of fear drop away but there is so much more unraveling to come.

The end of summer is nearing. Ricardo and I sit on a bridge one warm, August night, dangling our feet over the edge. We're watching a spider precisely weave its web of fine silken thread. Taking my hand in his, Ricardo turns to me and says, "I'm ready to take the leap. Earlier this spring, I prayed for someone to share my life with and to create this vision. I know you're that someone. We both share the same vision, and I've always wanted a family." His eyes meet mine, searching for an answer. I'm at a loss for words. I'm overwhelmed with joy to the point I'm speechless. I nod yes as tears pool in my eyes. He pulls me into his arms. Since we've both been married before, we're more interested in a union of our souls, an alchemical blending and less about a traditional marriage.

I need a strong man to walk this path with. Ricardo isn't afraid to speak his mind and call me out on my own issues. He isn't going to try to be someone he isn't nor sugar coat the way he feels about things. He isn't afraid of my passion or my anger. I've had too many men in my life that turned away from me when I was angry. I like that Ricardo doesn't run from my fury, in fact, most of the time he joins right in.

Chapter 9
Little One

*Little one, how you've changed my life, stretching me to be-
come more of who I am. Your little angel wings that carry you
through your day, with tender feet that will never touch the ground,
leave a print in the sand nor wear a hole in a pair of old sneakers.
You are the harbinger of peace.*

Ricardo and I've been together for about six months now. It's
the end of summer, and he's still at his summer camp. Lying in bed,
I open my eyes but am barely awake, that in between time where
the veil to the other worlds has yet to drop concealing the realm of
magic. To my left I feel a large presence, not really in a particular
form, but I know he's big, and I know he's male.

"Hello, mother," he says in a rather commanding voice. I intuitively know he's introducing himself to me as my future son.

"Hello. Don't come in too soon. Ricardo and I need time to get
to know one another," I respond.

"HAHAHAHA," he lets out a hearty laugh and says, "You two
are cemented together," and then he's gone.

His visit is short and to the point. A lengthy conversation is not
in order. He flew in, said hello, and my immediate thought is that
it's too soon in our relationship to have a child together, and I'm
not sure I want to have any more children.

I pull my down comforter up over my head to block out the morning sun and give myself some time to contemplate.

"Wow, that was weird."

He felt so much like Ricardo. He had the same type of masculine strength and clarity. And I definitely detected sarcasm when he laughed. That was so much like Ricardo, too.

While I'm certain he's planning on coming into the world as my son, as the weeks pass, I dismiss his visit. My experiences of the unseen world retain a dream-like quality, and I don't trust them enough to let them inform my day to day actions. Eventually, the elusive messages become an undeniable physical reality, and I think to myself, *oh yeah, I remember getting that message.*

It's the beginning of September and Ricardo had spent the past few weeks closing up his summer camp. He signed up for a basketball workshop at Omega Institute and asks me to join him for the weekend. The kids are visiting their dad, so I look over the schedule of classes. The only class I'm interested in is one on tantra. It feels odd to go to a class on tantra without my partner, but it's a last minute decision. We agree to meet there.

Omega Institute, a retreat center in Rhinebeck, NY, is only a couple hours from my home. I've never been there before, but have heard a lot about it. It hosts many well-known spiritual teachers and thought leaders and has a steady flow of people from NYC attending.

I arrive at Omega, and after parking and grabbing my small bag, I head to their bookstore where I'm meeting Ricardo. I spot him in the back, bent over a book he's reading intently. My heart skips a beat as soon as I see him. I stop to look at him. He feels like home —wearing an old, worn-out t-shirt with faded jeans. He's interesting, laid-back and loves nature, but he's also intensely smart and well-read on just about every topic.

"Hey," I say resting my hand on his back not wanting to interrupt his reading.

"Oh hey, you made it," he says smiling, leaning over to kiss me.

Small moments like this warm my heart and help to heal the memories of walking into my ex-husband's home office. No matter what, the children and I were always an intrusion.

Taking my bag and flinging it over his shoulder, I follow him to our cute, little cabin that's just down the path from the main area, tucked in the woods and shaded by several large oak trees.

The next morning comes early, and we both have a full day of classes ahead of us.

"I'll meet you in the cafeteria for dinner as soon as my class is over," I say as we quickly hug and go off in separate directions to our classes. The tantra class has about 20 people, both men and women. I'm surprised to find very few couples attending. As the female leader of the class begins to talk about the history of tantra, I look around the room at the different participants. There's an older woman who constantly fixes her hair and adjusts her shirt, making sure her cleavage is revealed while she glances and smiles at some of the men near her. My heart goes out to her. I guess she's probably around 60 years old, and I wonder about her personal story. Our culture has been so infused with continual messaging that a woman's ability to attract a man by looks alone is her main asset.

A few of the men's eyes continually dart around the room as if searching for a mate. They remind me of the wild turkeys behind our house. The kids and I are always amused watching the males during mating season strutting about with their tails fully fanned, flaunting themselves in front of all the females. These men may not have a full plumage of feathers, but their muscle flexing is one and the same.

As I listen to the instructors describe some of the exercises we'll be doing, I wish I had given this class a little more thought before signing up. The exercises involve massage and other forms of bodily contact with a partner. I don't feel emotional safety is held in high regard.

The class becomes an exercise for me to practice healthy boundaries. Years ago, I would have fled from this experience as my only option, for fear setting boundaries might offend someone. As the teacher gives an overview of the class, I take the time to be really present with my comfort zone. I feel pressure to follow the teacher's instructions, pressure from my class partner and pressure from wanting to do right by myself.

When the teacher announces it's time to choose our partners, I shrink, trying to make myself invisible. But from the other side of the room, I see a tall, dark haired man walking towards me. His eyes fixed on me.

Okay, well here it goes. You can't shrink back anymore, or you'll never be able to clearly set your boundaries.

"Hey there, I'm Trista," I say with every ounce of forced confidence and enthusiasm.

"Hi, I'm Rob," he says, seemingly taken aback by my sudden forwardness.

"I know the teacher says we're supposed to take turns and lie on top of one another, but that's not comfortable for me, so let's just sit and talk," I say keeping eye contact with him.

"Oh, well, I'm not sure we can do the exercise that way," he says awkwardly.

"You're welcome to find another partner," I say smiling.

He graciously accepts my terms, and we have a really beautiful time sharing with one another.

I'm so relieved when the class is over and dart out of the room to meet Ricardo for dinner. He has a good laugh as I share my experience with him. We finish our meal and head back to our cozy cabin in the woods.

We listen to the owls hooting and the frequent rustling of leaves outside our window as we lay in bed together, our bodies intertwined. The moon is almost full, its soft, silvery light casting shadows of tall trees and turning the dew drops of the night air into twinkling, little stars. We make love, I on top of him as waves of passion ripple through my body like a swift flowing river. I'm overwhelmed with love. It's like liquid gold pouring over the two of us mending any cracks or brokenness, dissolving all boundaries until we become one. When he comes, I hear a message.

"You need to pull him in."

I intuitively know that it's my son I'm to pull in. In my mind, I reach my hand up into the starry heavens and pull Javier, my son, in. It feels like my spirit body reaching high up, stretching to the stars and pulling in his spirit.

Enraptured with our love making, I'm not fully aware of what I've just done, but later the next day, as I sit on the bed, I feel the moment of creation, a subtle burst of energy, two opposing forces coming together in union deep in my belly. But I question it, dismiss it and go on with my day.

Two months later, my pregnancy is confirmed.

It isn't a joyous occasion for me. Matthew and Jessi have just reached ages where I have a glimpse of more independence, and now, I'm starting all over again. But that isn't the worst of it. My fear of being pregnant without taking the traditional path of marriage shocks even myself. Impressed upon me by my parents throughout my teenage years, pregnancy without marriage is the most devastating, most shameful thing that can ever happen to our family. Far worse than a terminal illness.

As the only daughter in the family, I carried this responsibility for my family's well-being, walking a very thin tight rope between managing their fear of sex and my blossoming sexuality. There were times where I succumbed to the fires of passion with my boyfriend, but fear always yanked me out of the moment just in time, like a cold pale of water dousing a fire. Getting pregnant would have been an irreversible mistake that would have brought down the whole family into the underworld of shame.

I grew up with this fear, and now, here it is, staring me in the face.

Panicked, I imagine myself walking around town displaying the red letter of shame while everyone glares at me with their judgmental looks.

So instead of tears of joy, I cry tears of sorrow. I feel completely alone. I don't like that I'm so afraid of being judged. I want to believe I'm strong and care little of what my family or community thinks. But it's just not so. As hard as I try to shed the old beliefs ingrained in me by my family and our church, they're undeniably a part of me. I want to tear at them, shred them, burn them. Why do I feel so entwined with threads of beliefs that are not mine?

A conversation amongst the ladies of my family's church persists, playing in my head over and over again.

"Did you hear about the Haggerty girl?"

"No, what's happened, is she ill?"

"No, worse, she's pregnant and not married."

I fall to my knees, sobbing, clutching a Black Madonna statue I brought back with me from France. Tears for every woman who's carried shame projected on to her by society. Tears for every woman who feared she's done wrong in the face of love. Tears for all the children born into a harsh world.

Please mother. Free me from these chains. They are not mine. Empty my womb of shame and fear and fill it only with light and love for this child. Help me to stand in my power and carry this child like only a Goddess would do.

I remember "meeting" the spirit of my child a couple months ago in my bedroom — how incredibly strong he felt to me, like the type of person that was going to do whatever he wanted to do, caring very little with what others thought. I remember the power I felt pulling him from the stars.

My spine begins to shiver, and my heart beats faster. The Divine Mother rises up inside of me, her alchemical power transforming shame into pride, panic into grace and fear into love. Taller and stronger in spirit, I'm not going to let the fears and beliefs of others taint my experience of birthing this beautiful baby.

I think of the church and the story of Mother Mary and her immaculate conception as an unwed woman. I peel back the wrongful myths and stories told as facts by the church. Their stories don't ring true to me. They feel purposefully contrived to portray the ideal woman and mother as pure and unobtainable. An archetype that has influenced the hearts and minds of women who strive to be as pure as she, denying their passion and desire for pleasure.

I go to my bookshelf lined with books that Helena recommended to me over the years. Many I haven't found the time to read, but I pull one off the shelf regarding Egypt. I pour through it and find a section on Mother Mary and Magdalena — both high priestesses of Isis. I come to my own conclusion that their pregnancies were most likely carefully planned births carrying the bloodline of the grail kings, despite the fact they lived in a time where women had few rights.

"I like this story better," I say to myself.

I call Ricardo as soon as I feel more settled. He's in California visiting his family and is super excited with the news. He had a dream a year before where he saw himself with a son and is completely on board. He moves into my home with the three of us and is a fully involved father-to-be. The kids are thrilled, too, that they're going to have a little brother or sister. Ricardo makes me eat every kind of vegetable imaginable, and I feel healthy and strong. His excitement and care gives me even more strength and courage.

I told my parents over the phone but had avoided seeing them in person. One day, my mom stops by when she knows Ricardo is away.

"I can't believe you are doing this to us," she says with an unforgiving expression.

"This isn't about you, mom. This is about me. I'm going to have a healthy and happy pregnancy. And if you're going to let your beliefs get in the way, then I won't have you involved," I say with complete confidence. Something that just weeks prior, I don't think I would have been able to say.

She says nothing and gets up and leaves and never mentions it again.

We find a midwife, Eleanor, nearby where we go for my monthly, pregnancy checkups. We plan a home birth, and everything is going well. On one visit, I'm standing in Eleanor's kitchen scheduling our next visit, when I notice a magazine lying on her counter, a Christian publication. I feel a subtle pang in my gut and glance over at her. Our eyes meet momentarily as if we're thinking the same thing but not speaking the words. She never mentions it, and I never ask if our not being practicing Christians will inhibit her ability to tend to my care.

During my last month of pregnancy, on a hot summer's day, Ricardo and I drive down a dirt road that has the illusion of disappearing into the hill to look at a piece of property. We want to find a large piece of land for moving his camp and for creating our vision together. A friend tells us about a parcel of land for sale that's just 15 minutes away from my house. The dirt road stretches endlessly between two fields and looks more like a pathway for a farm tractor. We cross a tiny bridge over a meandering stream that disappears into cascading willows, past an old gravel pit and up over a small knoll. On the other side is the property. 200 acres of fields and woods set way back against the valley hills. There's an old farmhouse, two very old, yet charming barns, discarded, rusty farm equipment and broken down cars scattered about, barely visible above the overgrown burdock and honeysuckle bushes. The house, deserted for years, has been vandalized. Its windows smashed and cupboards torn out. A pretty awful sight.

The realtor, her expression apologetic, greets us. When she sees me nine months pregnant, she looks even more apologetic at the condition of the property. I imagine she dropped the price considerably thinking no pregnant woman would ever want to move into such a dilapidated, old house. But what she doesn't know is that we don't really care anything about that. We are more interested in the land. We explore the narrow farm trails and footpaths that call us deeper into the woods. There is definitely a magical feel to the land that's palpable. We easily disregard all the junk scattered about.

The land invites us to explore in a way I've never experienced. I think back to my sacred journey to the stone circles and the Sidhe. I feel them welcoming us here. The bushes and the trees and the winding footpaths sparkle in the sun. Everything appears greener and more vibrant and alive — the shimmer and the shine that I remember some of the Irish and Scottish stories describe. I know it's a magical landscape. We make our offer and to our surprise, the realtor accepts it without hesitation. This is going to be the new home for Hawk Circle, and eventually our home, too.

A week later, I'm bent over my tomato plants, weeding in our garden. The summer sun beats down on my back. My water broke earlier in the day, and my contractions are slow to come. I hope squatting in the garden and doing some weeding might help get things moving. It reminds me of the images of goddesses squatting and giving birth that I'd seen chiseled onto cave walls. The kids are across the road at their grandparents', giving me the space to focus. Everything is ready for a home birth, and Ricardo and I are very excited. He's been so attentive through the whole pregnancy, taking me to the midwife every month, cooking healthy meals for me and rubbing my aching back at times when I'm uncomfortable.

I'm happy to redo my pregnancy experience with him. My other two pregnancies were happy and healthy, but I was alone. My ex-husband was always working so I went to my doctor appointments by myself. When I was in labor, I remember having to ask him to turn off the ball game. Knowing nothing different, I accepted his behavior as normal. The contrast of Ricardo's tender care shines a light on my past experience. Now I know what having a true birthing partner is like.

My contractions come more quickly, and I reach for Bradford, who stands nearby as I'm weeding. Using him as support, I stand up and waddle into the house. My other two labors were both long and super hard, and I anticipate the same. When Eleanore arrives, Ricardo and I are upstairs in the bedroom, and Kelly, who's downstairs, shows her the way to our room. She walks into our bedroom, smiling and greeting us, and then her eyes dart to the wall behind me where I have several papier mache masks that I had made on display. One is my "Black Madonna" mask I painted black and embedded with brightly colored jewels. They're beautiful, but the midwife's smile becomes forced and her disposition shifts. I note this but return my focus to my labor.

Hours pass and my contractions are still starting and stopping. I know I'm getting close to the danger zone and the risk of infection. My water broke several hours ago. While everyone is downstairs, I take some time to pray and ask for guidance. I'm getting more and more concerned with my labor. My awareness keeps going to my little one's head. There's something not right. I sit on the floor with my back against my bed, and reach for my Black Madonna statue, a small, dark wooden figurine that I had bought in Limoux, France that stands on the table next to my bed. I hold her to my heart.

"Mother, I need your guidance. Something feels wrong. Please keep my baby safe."

As I'm praying, Eleanor walks in. Her eyes dart to the statue I hold in my hands.

"Oh, can you wait a minute? Will you stop what you're doing for a second?" she asks, with apparent concern in her eyes as she quickly leaves the room.

"Okay," I say hesitantly, not really sure why.

Minutes later, Eleanor re-enters, wearing a simple scarf on her head. Her expression, once kind, shifts to hardheartedness.

"I'm afraid you're praying to the wrong person," Eleanor says quite sternly.

"I'm not sure I understand what you're talking about," I respond feeling the heat of rage rise up inside of me. I know exactly what she's talking about.

"Well, you should be praying to Jesus," she says so matter-of-factly, her eyes turning a steel-blue, icy color.

I am so angry and yet so vulnerable. Both Ricardo and Kelly are downstairs and know nothing of what is going on. If Ricardo was here, he would, without a doubt, be furious as well. But I'm alone and the mother bear in me wants to tear her to shreds with my words. My mind reels with all the possible ways this can go down but remind myself that I'm in labor.

Choosing my words very carefully, I say, "Well, I'm praying to Jesus' mother," careful not to refer to her as the Black Madonna. "Being a mother herself, I feel she better understands my concern in this moment more so than Jesus," I add, concealing my rage.

"Well, she was just a woman," says Eleanor.

WHAT THE FUCK? Did she just actually just say that? And she's a midwife? Who the hell does she think she is? Is she actually going to put her religious bullshit duty in front of her commitment to being my midwife? And start telling me who I should be praying to?

I am enraged and shocked. Now, the reason for her shift in energy earlier in the day when she walked into the bedroom and saw my masks is clear. In her mind, she's doing the Lord's work in the house of the Devil.

Everything feels like it's in slow motion. I continue to hold my Black Madonna statue in front of my big, round belly. I'm in labor, and I need her, and I know this. But I also want to tear away her ignorance and condemning beliefs. How dare she tell me I'm praying to the wrong person. How dare she impose her religious bullshit on me in my home. I draw in a deep breath, center myself and allow my awareness to expand beyond the fringes of my physical reality. I see in the periphery of my vision, a circle of goddesses dancing around me, telling me to let it go. They're here with me. They dance with such joy. It's the only thing that gets me through this moment. I continue to hold the Black Madonna, and fortunately Kelly walks in and interrupts the inquisition. We change the subject to my needing to go to the hospital since my water broke so long ago, and I'm making little headway with my contractions. I'm relieved to go to the hospital and be under someone else's care.

Hours later and into the next day, I'm still in labor. Remembering this little one's large spirit, I keep trying to tune in and communicate with him. Something still doesn't feel right to me. Ricardo is behind me, squatting in the narrow hospital bed, getting increasingly more agitated as he witnesses my incredible pain without apparent progress. Hours ago, the nurses had put me on Pitocin to strengthen my contractions. Each one is a freight train moving through me. It's impossible to "ride the waves" because there's no rhythmic movement to them, no natural ebb and flow. I breathe through each contraction and collapse into Ricardo's arms, barely able to move or stay awake.

After hours of this, the nurses discover he's breach and so far into the birth canal, there's no turning him around. They prepare me for a C-section and I'm relieved a decision has been made. Ricardo never leaves my side the whole time. We both watch from behind the curtain they drape between me and my belly, eagerly anticipating the birth of our child. As much as I wanted a home birth and at the very least, a natural birth, I'm so relieved to be out of pain. It's been two days, and I'm exhausted. But as they deliver our baby, I notice the concerned looks the doctor and nurses give to one another. Their eyes catching each other's glances, the unspoken words and the forced smiles.

What's happening? Why the awkward looks?

They wrap him in a towel and bring him over and show us his beautiful, round, baby face with brown eyes that look just like Ricardo's. With hesitation, they also turn him over and show us his open spine at the base. All color drains from Ricardo's face as he collapses to the floor. I feel completely peaceful, or maybe it's the exhaustion. I look at his little spine and can see the opening at the base. I know the power of this child's spirit and know that whatever way he comes into this world is by his own design.

His appearance in my bedroom last summer was a gift. He felt so powerful. He's an experienced magician. Not the kind that pulls a rabbit out of the hat at a child's birthday party. No, he's the kind of magician that shapes reality and can influence the world around him by supernatural means. That's who he is to me and in this moment, I cling to this belief as both his and my lifeline. Javier is okay. He chose this and I am going to do whatever I can to support him on his path.

The next hour or so is a whirlwind. We're rushed to a larger hospital an hour away. Javier has what medical professionals call spina bifida. His spine is open at the base and requires surgery to stitch it closed. A team of neurosurgeons are already waiting for him. It all happens so quickly and it's going to take days, maybe weeks for it to all sink in.

I'm stuck in my hospital bed, recovering from the C-section for what feels like an eternity. Ricardo helps me in and out of bed, careful not to move me too quickly with the searing pain in my abdomen. I keep reminding him not to crack any jokes that will make me laugh because it hurts terribly, although, it's a blessing that we're laughing at all. We spend a whole week in the ICU, Ricardo steadying me so I can hold our son and nurse him. We're just going through the motions of what needs to be done, even as we struggle to comprehend the ramifications of Javier's health.

At one point, I'm sitting in the ICU while Javi sleeps and Ricardo has gone to the cafeteria. A team of young residents, led by an older, serious-looking doctor heads towards Javi disregarding my presence. I glance at a nurse standing in the back of the room, and our eyes meet. She shakes her head and mouths the word "no" just as I see the doctor start to pick Javi up by his tiny hands and drop him back in the bed as a way to demonstrate nerve response in a baby with spina bifida. Clutching the arms of the chair, I push myself up quickly, my insides flinching with burning abdominal pain.

"You're not touching my baby," I say. The doctor ignores me.

"You're not touching my baby," I say louder.

"I'm just demonstrating....," he starts to say.

"Not on my baby. I'm his mother!" I say, mustering up all the energy I can.

He takes his team and walks on. I glance over at the nurse, and she smiles nodding her head. I'm so grateful for her. I'm short on energy trying to heal, along with nursing and trying to comprehend all that is going on.

My parents, Ricardo's mom, and at other times, Kelly come to visit and bring Matthew and Jessi to see me and to meet their little brother. Seeing them is like inhaling a breath of fresh air.

One day the phone rings in my hospital room. It's Helena. Hearing her voice on the other end, calling me Boobala in her German accent and telling me I need to eat hot fudge and anything gooey is so comforting.

"Food for the soul sweetie!" she says.

She can "see" Javier's strength of spirit and talks about him in such an honoring way. I'm so reassured by this. I've encountered too many of the "I feel so sorry for you," look and it's so disempowering. How do looks and words of pity serve anyone?

What I need to hear is, "You've got this!" or "If there's anyone who can figure this out, it's you."

Thankfully, I get this from Helena.

The next day we're discharged. I can't wait to get home and wash off the smell of the hospital, cook our own good food and sleep in our own bed. You can get fixed in a hospital, but you can't heal. I need to smell the outdoors, lay in the grass and feel the sun.

According to the doctors, Javier will never walk, but I don't want to raise him projecting these limitations. Children are so susceptible to what their parents think about them and take it on as their own truth. I don't want to do this to Javier. I don't want to raise him with all his possible limitations at the forefront of my mind. He's beautiful and perfect just the way he is, and his doting brother and sister think so, too.

As much as a gift Javi is for our whole family, his birth spirals us into a slow, ongoing state of trauma. I'm thankful he's my third child — the care and tending to his needs as a baby are second nature to me. For Ricardo, it's more difficult. He's a first-time father with too much on his plate. Moving into a ready-made family, having his first child born with special needs, buying land for the first time, and preparing to move his business is too much all at once. A river of chaos flows through our life, knocking everything over, leaving us wondering if we're ever going to find our footing. He does the best he can at managing it all, but it's traumatic for him in many ways.

These first few months with Javi put us in an automatic state of hyper-vigilance. Children with spina bifida are at risk of having fluid retention on their brain. One day he takes an extra-long nap. I'm partly relieved that I have extra time to wash and fold the laundry. But something nags at me. I can't enjoy his extra long nap. When he wakes, I watch him like a hawk for the rest of the day. He seems okay, but sure enough, in the middle of the night, Javier starts having seizures. We rush him to the hospital where they determine he has fluid built-up in his head. Handing him over to the doctor, my arms are empty. I turn to hold Ricardo's arm as an attempt to fill the void. My tear-filled eyes plead with the doctor to save my son and return him to my arms, but I find no assurance by his furrowed brow and swift action. The nurses and doctor rush him away and the doors close behind them. All we can do is wait.

The waiting room is a cold and empty space — void of any comfort. Plain white walls, simple chairs with hard vinyl cushions, nothing to soothe my frazzled nerves. Ricardo and I sit, staring quietly out a small window. All I hear is the buzzing of the fluorescent lights overhead. I push away intruding thoughts of the doctor entering the room with a grief stricken expression.

Don't you dare take him from me. I won't let you. I refuse to lose a child! This door is CLOSED!

Hours later, what feels like an eternity, I hear the door to the waiting room open. *What expression am I going to be met with. Is my heart going to be crushed or am I going to cry tears of joy?* Both Ricardo and I hesitantly turn, and there she is, the glowing and smiling face of a nurse — an expression that can only bear good news. Tears of relief emerge from my already swollen eyes, and I dart to the bathroom as nausea overcomes me. I vomit out the fear, the stress, the worry and thank the goddess for saving my son.

Our taxing summer is coming to an end. Ricardo is busy with his usual, end-of-the summer ritual of closing up his summer camp. He's barely been there during the summer, running back and forth between camp and home. Fortunately, he hired wonderful staff that were able to take over during his absence. I take Matthew and Jessi school shopping, and am just walking through the door, carrying Javi, when the phone rings.

"Hello?"

"Hi Trista? It's Eleanor." Hearing her voice brings on my forgotten rage like a tsunami rising out of a calm sea.

"Yes?" I respond through clenched teeth.

"How are you? How's Javier?" she asks in a friendly way. She never came back to our house for a visit to check on him as is custom protocol with midwives, nor did she call to see how his surgery was right after birth. I hadn't talked to her since the night I had my C-section.

"Fine."

"Oh good. I'm so glad to hear that. Listen, I'm wondering if you can help me with something? I'm being brought up on legal charges at the hospital where I work in Delaware County, and I'm wondering if you'd be willing to testify on my behalf?"

Time stands stills. The few seconds that pass feel like an eternity. The moment where a past wrong is made right. Maybe it's karma? Where once I had no voice, but now I do?

"Eleanor, you wouldn't want me on the stand," I say calmly.

"Oh? Why's that?" she asks, bewildered.

"Can you hold for a minute?" I ask.

"Oh, of course," she says.

"Here you go, sweetie," I say to Javi as I tuck him into his little bed in the next room. I don't want to hold him while having this conversation for fear my mounting anger will scare him.

"Eleanor?" I snap, returning to the phone.

"Yes, I'm here," she responds.

"You don't want me to testify on your behalf because I would make sure you lost this case," I say very clearly.

"Why? I don't understand?" she says, stumbling on her words from apparent unease.

Really?

"Why? Because you came into my home as my midwife, while I was in labor, and started telling me who I should and shouldn't be praying to. I did NOT hire you to be my spiritual advisor. I hired you to be my midwife. How dare you put my baby and me at risk while you took on the role as a preacher? Never once, in all the 8 months I had been coming to you, did you ever mention that your religious views would get in the way of your being a midwife. The subject never came up. If it was up to me, I'd make sure you never practiced midwifery or nursing ever again. So, the answer is NO. I will not testify on your behalf and consider yourself lucky that I'm not the one pressing charges," I say, and with that, I hang up, my hands shaking with rage.

Matthew and Jessi stare at me wide-eyed. I take a deep breath and soften my gaze, and smile at them.

"Sometimes you just have to speak your mind," I say, giving them a wink. Matthew gives me a sideways grin, and Jessi, who never has a problem letting others know what she's thinking shouts, "Yeah! You tell her, mommy!"

Over the next several months, Ricardo and I grow more confident with our care for Javi, but still, with ongoing concern. I'm home with him the most, and reap the gifts he brings, but also bear the brunt of the responsibility. He is so easy going, sleeps well through the night and has a deep belly laugh that makes everyone smile. His presence alone resets my nervous system. When he's in a roomful of people, sitting in his baby seat, he moves his little fingers in such a way that I swear he's reweaving the energy in the room. Only when there's lots of people gathered does he do this. It's also apparent to me that he sees beyond the veil. I'll catch him looking into space as though he's watching someone and then laugh hysterically.

He loves watching Jessi make faces and jump up and down, and he also welcomes Matthew's calm and tender presence. Sometimes I just want to close the door on the rest of the world and preserve some sense of normalcy, but I can't. There are doctors that oversee his progress and there are special need advocates that come visit discussing therapies he'll need as he gets older. And well-intended public health nurses that stop by to see how he's doing. I just want to scream. *Will you PLEASE just get out of our lives!* But I have to surrender to what is.

I was so close to having more freedom as Matthew and Jessi were getting older, but now freedom feels a lifetime away. I spend my days breastfeeding, changing diapers, massaging his legs, packing school lunches for Matthew and Jessi. If things were different, Javi would be crawling by now, maybe even getting ready to walk, or at least pulling himself up to a standing position. But this isn't the case. His sedentary physicality becomes mine. And I can't help but feel jealous of Ricardo's freedom of going over to our new land with Hawk Circle staff and building and fixing and cleaning things up. Working towards something. Feeling a sense of accomplishment at the end of the day. Instead, my days are slowed to the pace of a caterpillar. The clock ticks and ticks and ticks — time moving so slow. I'm forced to sit with my feelings. Forced to surrender.

Every day I make the conscious choice to tend to Javi's needs with grace. I'm tending the soul of another. *There's honor in that, right? This is a sacred act.* I have to believe this, because there are plenty of moments the path of resentment taunts me, marked by a neon sign. But no, I won't let myself walk down that road even for a few minutes.

I'm painfully aware of Javi's undetermined future. Little socks that never dirty, and pants that never wear at the knees. Daily observations that remind me I'm dealing with a very different situation then when raising Matthew and Jessi. I'm reminded during insignificant moments, like folding the laundry.

Spontaneous visits from friends with their kids have stopped. I figure they either don't know how to respond to my situation, or maybe they feel guilty that their babies who are near the same age as Javi are already walking or doing things that Javi may never do. Kelly is the only friend that continues to stop by. She adores Javi, and I appreciate her visits so much.

There are days where I feel like I did back in the cave in France — helpless. I am finding my way through another kind of darkness. I can't see too far in front of me, and I have no idea what's around the corner. This is the primordial mother's cauldron. The womb, the cocoon where there's stillness and all I can do is surrender.

Chapter 10
Journey to the Underworld

It's dark down here. I don't like it. I feel like I'm Alice in Wonderland falling down the rabbit hole. Falling, falling, losing all sense of control. There are mad hatters everywhere, but we're not having a tea party, nor is there any friendly rabbit. Seems like every path I take is met with another demon and another. I try to reach for some sort of handle, some way to catch myself and keep myself from further falling into the darkness of the underworld, but every time I do, it comes loose, falls apart, and I'm descending once again.

Our challenges with Javi during his first year spills into the next. There are more emergency visits to the hospital, and everyday I'm afraid I'm going to lose him. Ricardo and I desperately want stability, but instead a tornado is tearing our life apart and scattering the pieces far and wide. The upheaval brings to the forefront every attachment and control issue we have.

Ricardo continues to work without respite on our new land while moving his business, creating a new home and parenting a child with special needs. The stress he endures overwhelms him like a recurring tidal wave. I reach out to him, searching for reassurance for myself when fears of losing both Javi and him penetrate.

When I quiet my mind, and listen to my heart, the message is clear. Breathe through it. Let go of my fears. But so often, I feel if I let go, I'll lose everything, including myself.

Twice, I receive a phone call from my ex-husband threatening to take the kids, his way of exerting power and control that has more to do with his unresolved anger towards me than his desire to be an involved father. Staying grounded and centered is the only thing I can do, but I repeatedly fail. More often than not, I'm flattened by the tidal wave of chaos and uncertainty.

One night after the kids are in bed and sound asleep, Ricardo and I sit together curled up next to the wood stove, a priceless moment of reprieve. He shares some of the things he's struggling with, and by the way he carefully chooses his words, I know this is a vulnerable moment for him. I'm thrilled we have some time for the two of us and that he's willing to open up and share. As he talks, I keep reminding myself to keep my mouth shut, not to analyze, not try to fix it, just stay quiet and listen.

There's a pattern that has come up for me in previous relationships and it has to do with forms of sexual expression that I grew up believing are taboo. I didn't feel safe enough to explore such intimate issues in my previous marriage, but Ricardo is different and he's asking for my help. I'm under the impression that I'm going to save him, but in the end, it's me I save. Exploring different expressions of sex with him feels like something I can do — maybe a part of my life that will take me away, at least momentarily, from the everyday stress.

But it doesn't come without fear.

I've been here before — a threshold moment. I can feel it. I just walked through a doorway, committed to an initiation that I'm sure is going to set many things in motion for me. I'm excited because at least it holds the promise of change. My feeling is confirmed by a dream I have the next night.

I'm standing in the backyard of my childhood home. I'm comforted seeing the familiar willow tree, the large evergreen hedge and our house right behind me. I notice the seed heads of the tall grass in the un-mowed field swaying back and forth as though an invisible force quickly moves towards me. Suddenly, from out of the edge of the field, a large, orange snake emerges. It's enormous, about fifteen feet long with a circumference the size of my leg. It moves swiftly towards me. I run, scrambling to seek refuge in our house, but the snake is too fast. It seizes me, sinking its sharp, pointy fangs through the delicate underside of my forearm. I drop to my knees as I scream with pain. It slithers away just as swiftly as it appeared. I look down at my arm and the bite of the snake spells out the word "carnal."

I wake up, startled, breathing heavily, and immediately pull my arm from the bed covers, rubbing my forearm, half expecting to find large puncture wounds from the snake. But no, just a dream. I relax and lie in bed, reviewing the details. I remember when I was little and how often I woke up in the middle of the night screaming as snakes slithered all over me.

I quietly slide out of bed, not wanting to wake Ricardo, and go over to my book shelf where I keep Ted Andrew's *Animals Speak* book. Tiptoeing down the hallway, I go into the bathroom, turn on the light and sit down on the floor to read. I read about snake medicine and how they hold the power of transmutation and represent the primal life force. They shed their skin, like us shedding our old beliefs and illusions and become reborn. I also know that carnal is having knowledge of the flesh. I think of the snake in the Garden of Eden and remember reading about the snake giving Eve the apple from The Tree of Knowledge. Not Satan, as Christianity proclaims, but the primal force that pulls us down into the human realm and the world of desire.

I have mixed feelings about all this, but I remember Helena saying, "When you have a dream where an animal seizes you, whatever initiation they oversee is an initiation you can't escape."

I know what this is. It's the initiation of the sexual priestess —the sacred whore. I had read about this in Sylvia Perera's book, *Descent to the Goddess*. A book that Helena recommended I read before going to France. It didn't make sense to me, and I put it on the shelf. But ever since I returned home from France, it became my bible.

Her book tells the myth of Inanna, Sumerian Queen of the Heavens, stepping off her throne in search of her sister, Ereshkigal, who's been banished to the Underworld.

The next night, the kids are asleep, Ricardo's sitting on the couch watching a movie. It's been a couple of weeks since our talk, and I'm ready to leap into the role of the sexual priestess. I quietly walk up behind him and lean over the back of the couch.

"Do you want to fuck me?" I whisper in his ear, while brushing my lips against the back of his neck. I feel his body quiver and he smiles.

Upstairs, in our bedroom, I slide off my jeans and unbutton my shirt, and neatly fold them, laying them on a chair. I take off my underwear and my bra and toss them in the wicker hamper. Next, I slide on a pair of black, lace stockings, a black leather garter and matching thong, and a black leather bra. Stepping into a pair of black high-heeled pumps I go over and stand in front of my dresser, my make-shift altar, and light several white candles, praying to the Goddess for guidance. I take some fragrant oil I bought in France and begin massaging it across my stomach and between my thighs and over my breasts that spill out of my bra. The sweet, yet earthy aroma takes on a life of its own, a seductress pulling me further into the role of the sexual priestess and sacred whore.

Ricardo walks slowly into our dimly lit bedroom. He looks at me, standing in front of the glowing candles revealing my power. His eyes soften with apparent reverence, greater than what I feel for myself since I question the ethics of what I'm doing. Am I in alignment with the sacredness of sexuality? I feel that my appearance alone gives Ricardo permission to release long pent up passion as his breath quickens. He reaches for me, his face flushed and pulls me to him as we enter into the realm of flesh. In this moment and others, I'm fully in charge of this domain, the world of desire, feeling my raw, feral-like power where the palpable, dense energy is there for my bidding, energy that I can wield like the magician herself. It scares me, but at the same time, I like it.

The sexual realm of leather and whips is a domain that previously, I found repulsive. Whenever I saw images of women dressed in leather lingerie, I winced, shuddered, and turned away. But embracing this aspect of myself and this domain, gives me insight into the pain of others who get stuck here. And my willingness to embrace what I viewed as ugly was the path to my finding beauty. Here was my "edge"— the place where opposites meet, where fear meets courage.

I lived my life with too many societal and spiritual constraints, believing in the religious messaging that the world of the flesh is somehow evil, and restricting my expression of my power. But now, I'm fully unleashing my wild self and abandoning all moral code.

While I experience a tremendous amount of freedom, I also experience fear. On a deep, intuitive level, I feel I've opened a forbidden door. My parents live right across the road, and I constantly close my curtains on the windows facing their house.

I remember my grandmother giving my brother and me each some money to buy our own Christmas presents one year. She wanted us to wrap our gifts and bring them to her home on

Christmas night so she could see what we bought for ourselves. She had grown past the age where she could get out and go shopping. I bought myself a drawing of a gray wolf and black raven. When I unwrapped it, proudly showing it to her, she gave me a look of disgust.

"I think black birds and wolves are evil," she responded. My grandmother is a very sweet, church-going Christian. Even for her, this was a strong response.

Memories of this moment and others with my mother and grandmother reveal to me why I had banished my primal self. The fear of the wild feminine power runs deep in my family. As with the inquisition, when many women of power — witches and healers — went into hiding in order to survive, the more earthy, primal aspects of the women in my family did the same. Their response was passed on to me. It's up to me to break this pattern, to free and to heal the primal feminine breaking the pattern for myself and my family's lineage.

I feel like two different people. One, like Ereshkigal, wild and ferocious, and another, my ego self, the daughter of the patriarchy raised with strict societal values. While I liberate the first, the second is dismantled.

The dismantling is the hard part. I don't realize how molded I am by beliefs until they are stripped away. As I unearth the part of me that has been banished and fully enter into the Underworld, I go from feeling powerful to experiencing the victimization of the feminine.

When Inanna enters the first gate of descent in search of Ereshikgal, she's disrobed of her queenly attire, symbolic of her ego. I, too, approach the gate with an air of self-importance like a privileged savior.

While I wear no queenly attire, my ego is peeled away at every gate I enter. One right after another. My golden "know it all" crown, my queenly robe made from the fabric of righteousness, my breast plate and golden girdle that protects me from seeing my own flaws and my countless jewels of judgment all stripped away. I feel the betrayal, and the rejection, and the abuse of the feminine at the hand of the patriarchy. The emotional pain is like having my chest ripped open and my heart pulled out, and then pulverized into a million pieces. My wild self shows no remorse. No compassion. No empathy.

My emotional pain rises to the surface through conversations and life happenings that are innocent and well-intended, but easily trigger me. One day, my well-intentioned Dad comes over to my house when I'm not home and mows my lawn for me. He mows over an area I had planted with wildflowers. At the sight of seeing the wild part of my lawn now mowed, I fly into a rage while at the same time, crumple to the floor in a heap of despair. Mowing my wildflowers feels like the manicuring of my wild nature.

With so many of these situations, I fight furiously against the emotions that are triggered. I hate feeling like a victim. I'm used to rising above such feelings, but I recognize, I feel righteous, deserving of more, that somehow, being raised educated and expected to succeed somehow means that I'm immune to such feelings. That I'm better than this. The daughter of the patriarch's almighty pride.

Over time, I learn that a descent into the Underworld isn't about fighting nor is it about exercising my will. A descent into the realm of the Dark Mother is about surrendering to the feelings that have been long buried and letting them wash through me. Hearing the message over and over again, "STOP FIGHTING!" I finally listen and surrender.

While I spend several months exploring this realm with Ricardo, the time comes when I know I need to return from the Underworld. One night, while making love, I feel the Dark Goddess rise through me. I feel her presence as my own. She is fierce. A palpable power — not of anger or aggression, but instead magnetic like earth's gravity. Without a doubt, I know I can draw Ricardo's soul from his body. I'm jolted by my own fear and quickly withdraw from our lovemaking. This is the Goddess' destructive side and I pull back, pledging to myself that I will never open myself to this aspect of her again. Like nature, she is a force that gives life and takes life without remorse. It's not good or bad, it just is.

Our experience is deeply erotic, but I know I could get lost in this realm with its powerful magnetism like a drug of pleasure. I feel it begin to take hold of me in a way I don't like. My mind is too consumed by eroticism, and so I pull myself from its claws and resist its allure.

Knowing when to pull away is a painful, but necessary part of the initiation and I mourn the loss of our erotic nights. But I know I need to return from the Underworld, to leave my black leather lingerie buried in the bottom of my dresser drawer.

I refer back to my book for guidance. In the myth of Inanna, her loyal servant, Ninshibur tends to the hearth doing basic chores everyday while Inanna is gone. She represents the one small part of ourselves that stays in the upper world maintaining a sense of order. She has no life of her own, other than to serve, taking care of things in the life above as the soul descends.

In the end, she is the one that saves Inanna and she's the one that saves me.

Chapter 11
The Primal Self

Climbing and climbing my way out of darkness. I reach for what little light I see, a small glimmer of hope. Like being raised from the dead, my first gasp of air, the breath of life, I return home, renewed, grateful for the Great Mother.

As with Ninshibur, a small part of me tends to everyday life. If it wasn't for the kids and Javi's diaper changes and feedings, I would be completely lost. I keep them in a protective bubble as they remain their happy, child-like selves while I'm going through this. I think I'm hiding what's going on inside of me pretty well, but one day, Jessi climbs up on the kitchen chair, reaches for my face with her little hands, stares right into my eyes and kisses me on the forehead. Even though she's only six years old, in this moment, she's my sister priestess letting me know that I'm going to be okay.

I'm relieved when Ricardo goes away for a week to teach a class in California. I want the space by myself to do more inner work.

I'm walking along a grassy hillside, heading to a cave. As I get near the entrance, I slow my steps, cautiously approaching the cave's opening. I encounter a wild haired, bony and naked, frightening old woman crouched down on the dirt floor of the cave. She is picking black beetles off the ground with her skinny fingers and putting them in her mouth. I hear the crunch, crunch, crunch as she bites down, one beetle at a time. She's in a catatonic state as she rocks back and forth with a glassy, lifeless stare. She detects my presence and suddenly comes alive, fully alert and ready to pounce. She comes at me snarling, foaming at the mouth. I know she wants me dead. Given the chance, she would hang me on a meat hook to die as Ereshkigal did to Inanna. Or maybe leave my body for the vultures to pick at my eyes and tear at my flesh. I refuse to leave the entrance to the cave. Whatever she dishes out I need to accept as my fate for having banished her in the first place.

This is my power, my primal self. She's a force to be reckoned with. Kind of what I'd expect if a wild animal was caged for too long. I realize, as in the meditation, that I'm pretty numb and the only time I come alive and find my voice and be passionate is when I'm being threatened. These are the only moments when I sense my power, fierceness and immense anger. Not in a constructive way, only destructive. I have to "flip" this experience. I need to transmute my power, release the anger and be mindful of finding my voice and feeling alive in moments other than when feeling threatened.

While Ricardo is gone, I adopt the physical appearance of my primal self. I don't comb my hair. I wear a black sweatshirt with a pair of old jeans that are ripped at the knees. I dress this way for the whole week. Standing outside the school with the other parents, waiting to pick up my kids while holding Javi, I'm quite the sight with an aura around me that clearly sends the message, "Don't come near me." I want to fully embody HER, fully give myself over to HER so I can eventually integrate her into my being.

I am so drained of energy. Some mornings I can barely get out of bed. I drag myself through the day making dinner, packing school lunches, nursing Javi, driving the kids to their soccer games and play dates, all the while anxiously waiting for nightfall so I can climb into bed and go to sleep. Ricardo leaves early every morning and heads over to our land. We have a couple of young men who help clean up all the junk, repair the old run-down farmhouse and build a camp site for moving Hawk Circle next summer.

I become concerned for my well-being as I'm increasingly tired. One evening, after the kids are in bed, I notice my drum, *Twin Moons,* sitting in the corner of my bedroom. The fall before getting pregnant with Javi, I spent the weekend with a shaman who is a master drum-maker. I made a sacred drum, after working all day preparing the deer hide. That night, after a ceremony where I called in the spirit of my drum, I had a dream where I saw my drum being birthed. I was standing on a beach and far out on the horizon, I saw the full moon rise up over the ocean. Behind it was another moon in its shadow. The name *Twin Moons* was spelled out on the glistening water. It was a magical experience. I kept her in a sheepskin case that someone had made for me. She's been in the same spot for the past two years where I walk by no longer noticing her, but now she calls to me, an undeniable presence. I kneel down on the floor and take her out of the sheepskin. Bradford joins me, resting his head on my lap. I run my hand along the smooth, honey-colored deer hide of the drum, looking at symbols I painted with my own menstrual blood. I pick up the wooden drum beater I carved out of a piece of cherry wood and notice the snake head that appeared as I was carving. I smile, "How appropriate."

I beat on my drum, feeling awkward at first like we just met, but soon settle into a nice, deep rhythm. Her sound nourishes me in a way that I desperately crave. The steady beat and the chant that flows through me feels like a call to return from the Underworld. I drum daily for the next two weeks. I drum and sing myself back from the land of the dead. Like Ninshibur, when sensing Inanna is in trouble, drums her back from the Underworld and inevitably saves her. I am returning, but the journey is far from over.

One morning, a little hummingbird flutters at my bathroom window, its eyes fixed on me. I hear in my mind its message, "You need to call Indigo." It flies away as quickly as it appeared.

Indigo is an older medicine woman I had met at a gathering that Ricardo and I hosted on our new land. She's the type of older woman who you know has gone through her fair share of struggle and has a twinkle in her eye as a result of it. She isn't afraid to say exactly what she's thinking. I call her later that day, telling her that a hummingbird told me to call. She's silent for a moment and then says, "We need to do a burial ceremony!" We make plans for her to come in just a few weeks.

I don't know how to prepare for the ceremony, since Indigo gave me no instruction other than to dig a "grave" at least three feet deep. The day before her arrival, I find a nice, secluded spot, nestled in amongst a cluster of white pine trees and dig my cere-monial grave.

It's a cold, wet fall day, and Indigo is arriving any moment. Kelly's coming over to help, too. When they both arrive, the three of us head down to the site, sloshing through puddles, trying to keep a blanket dry for me. We settle ourselves in the best we can, Kelly and Indigo both kneeling on blankets next to my grave. I take off all my clothes, wrap them in my raincoat and tuck them in at the base of the tree hoping they'll stay dry. I climb into my grave. The ground is cold and damp, sending shivers rippling through my naked body. I imagine worms inching their way through the dirt towards the warmth of my body and ground bugs crawling all over my skin. The only comfort I have is the woodsy, sweet scent of the white pine trees that stand nearby, towering over me like guardians of my grave.

Kelly and Indigo slowly and very deliberately cover me with cold, wet, dirt, making sure my eyes and mouth are protected by a piece of thin, silk fabric. A three foot grave doesn't really seem that deep, but having the dirt piled on top of me is so heavy, I can't move at all. I try to lift my arms or move my foot, but I'm pinned to the earth like Osiris nailed to the wooden coffin. The dirt is cold and wet, and I tremble beneath the weight of the soil. I hear Kelly and Indigo talking, but with my ears covered, their voices are muffled. I can't see anything since my eyes are covered by the scarf and a layer of dirt.

I am in the womb of the earth.

I attempt to relax my body to ease my shivering, but I begin gasping for air.

"I can't breathe! I can't breathe!" I say panicking.

"There's nothing covering your mouth but the silk," says Kelly, reassuringly.

"I can't, I can't, I can't breathe!" I say, fighting for air.

Kelly and Indigo both assure me that there is nothing blocking my mouth or nose, but I am struggling for air and with my arms buried, I can't do anything. I'm completely helpless and powerless. *FUCK! Just another experience where I have to surrender.*

So, I intentionally become very still, slowing my breath down to almost nothing and surrender to the experience. As I do, I see the spirit of a woman climbing out of my body.

"Bitch," she says looking at me with contempt before turning and walking away into the forest.

What the hell is this about?

After I see her walk away, I effortlessly slip into a very peaceful healing space and lay in the arms of Mother Earth, communing with Her as I'm cleansed. Just what I need — to be held by the Great Mother.

The whole experience lasts for about an hour. The burial restores me in many ways. I feel so invigorated, so alive coming up out of the grave. My body is covered with dirt and it's raining and cold, but I don't care. Kelly and Indigo wrap a wool blanket around me and give me a big hug.

The return of energy and light in my eyes is noticed by many friends who are close to me. I'm so grateful for the little humming-bird that came to my window and grateful for Indigo too.

While the burial cleansed me of Underworld attachments, my pelvis swells and pants that fit just a week ago, no longer do. I've taken on a toxic garbage dump and am concerned that I won't be able to clear my womb and transmute the energy fast enough before becoming ill.

The very next day, after the burial ceremony, I walk to the end of our road with Matthew and Jessi, while pushing Javi in a stroller to pick up our mail. As I pull out countless bills and a magazine, Helena's Sacred Journey brochure falls to the ground. I quickly bend down to pick it up. I hold it in my hands like it's my lifeline. Pushing the stroller with one hand and holding her brochure with the other, I skim through her trips. My heart skips a beat when I see her trip to Greece that reads, *Birthing Aphrodite*.

"Hi Helena! It's Trista." I can't wait to talk with her, and call her the moment I walk in the house. She's been so busy traveling, and we haven't talked in several months.

"Treeeesta, how are you?" she asks and I detect concern in her voice.

"I'm okay. I just read through your brochure and saw your trip to Greece. I know I need to be on this trip. It sounds incredibly healing," I say. Just saying the words brings more relief than I've felt in quite some time.

"Ahhh, yes. That would be a wonderful trip for you. It's very healing. Birthing Aphrodite," Helena says.

Helena and I talk for quite some time. Planning a sacred journey to Greece is just what I need. It's the most hope I've felt in the past two years since the chaos of Javi's emergency hospital visits and my descent to the Underworld.

Chapter 12
Birthing Aphrodite

*B**athing in the crystal blue waters of Aphrodite, I'm gently rocked back and forth, my body renewed with each undulation. I feel the cool water caressing my breasts and between my thighs. The Greek gods stand back, providing a circle of fierce protection while the goddesses do their work. I remember this place. I remember the cleansing rituals in the Mediterranean waters, my bare feet walking the stone floors of the temples and the beauty, the power and the mystery that lay between my legs as a gateway to the Divine.*

Sometimes our path requires us to pray hard, focused prayer, as I call it.

This is what I do on my trip to Greece — daily, focused prayer for healing my sexual priestess aspect and my womb. As part of a bedtime ritual, I pray. Over time it becomes robotic, but then there are times when there's an urgent need for a direct response and my prayer is intended for a specific outcome. This is one of those times. I need healing and I need it now.

Ricardo is rightfully concerned when I tell him I need to go to Greece. This is my first sacred journey since meeting him, and I'm not used to having to "check in" with anyone regarding my travels. I'm reluctant to tell him, knowing he isn't going to be happy about it.

"What if there's another emergency, and you're not here?" Ricardo says with apparent fear.

"I know. That would be incredibly scary for you, but I feel it's going to be okay," I say reassuringly.

"You're still nursing him, you can't go," he adds.

"I have almost eight months before I leave," I say.

"I don't think it'll work. You're just going to have to go another time," Ricardo says with such obstinacy.

"I'm consulting with you, not asking for your permission," I remind him, with mounting anger.

I don't want to worry Ricardo, but I feel I have to go for my own well-being. The inner work that I did in the Underworld was so intense, and my pelvis and womb continue to stay swollen and bloated. I need healing, and I want so desperately to connect with the sacred sexual power of Aphrodite. I assure him it will all work out, but he wants to know how, and that I can't answer. I know my way of intuitively making decisions that often defy all rational sense is hard for him to deal with. But I'm confident this will all work out and I have time to figure it out.

Over the course of the next few months, every time I check in with my intuition, I feel it's fine to keep nursing Javi and not offer him anything else. As the time for my departure nears, Javi starts rejecting my breast whenever I try to nurse him.

He knows I'm leaving.

He happily takes to a bottle. Everything falls into place as I sensed it would. Making sure the kids have what they need, their school schedule and play dates all mapped out on the calendar, my parents lined up to help and reassuring words for Ricardo, I pack my bags for Greece. Leaving my family never gets easier, but as a mom, holding so much responsibility, taking time for myself, my work and my healing is necessary.

I arrive in Athens early the next morning. As the plane circles over the ancient city, preparing to land, I see the scintillating blue waters of the Mediterranean. The white homes with red, clay roofs scattered across the hillsides, provide a striking contrast to the deep, blue water. I instantly fall in love with this culture. The whole scene is renewing me, and I drink it into my parched soul. This is the birthplace of Aphrodite and the land of the Snake Goddess. What better place to find healing after spending many months in the Underworld?

After a brief, one-night stay in Athens, our group squeezes into a small airplane that when flying, sounds like the deafening whine of a vacuum cleaner. Peering through the tiny window, I see below the Greek islands, irregular blotches of green scattered throughout the brilliant blue Mediterranean. Moments later, we land in Crete, home to the ancient Minoan people who built Knossos, a remarkable palace in 7000BCE, a goddess-worshipping civilization that held many ritualistic celebrations with music, dance and games.

We settle into our newly-built hotel by the sea where we spend an entire week. A long wooden dock extends out into the water. Every morning, I wake up early, walk down to the very end of the dock and offer dried sage and rose petals from a leather pouch that Ricardo made for me. It's my gift to the gods and goddesses of Greece, particularly, Aphrodite. This is when I pray hard.

Dearest Gods and Goddesses, I need your help. I've come for healing and renewal. And I've come to unite with my dark haired sister, the priestess. Please guide me on this journey. Please grace me with your presence. Please provide me with healing. I fear I won't be well if I don't receive healing soon. I have three little ones who count on me. Please, I'm begging you to help me heal.

I repeat these words over and over again until they become as familiar to me as my own breath — every morning, every evening and many times in between. There are times I swear I feel Poseidon rising up out of the sea with his mighty trident in his hand. This area of the world is so connected to the gods and goddesses. They've been kept alive by the culture all this time.

I've been working with my sexual energy during my Underworld descent and in the process, I unearthed shame that is gripped by darkness. Shame for times I misused my sexual power and dishonored the sacred sexual priestess. Intense shame for memories of enduring sexual harassment and abuse. Some of the memories are from this lifetime, but there are layers upon layers of memories from lives lived in ancient times. The emotional pain is crippling.

I also have a dream.

I'm in a laundry room folding clothes and in walks a woman with long dark hair. She's sensual, alluring and feels so grounded. I back away, feeling uneasy and unsure I can trust her. She starts talking with me very nonchalantly, and I soon come to the conclusion that she's very kind and genuine.

Now, more than anything, I want to heal the ravine between us that I've created from my own judgement and fear. I've done so much work embracing this aspect of myself and now, all I can do is pray for healing.

On our first day in Crete, I'm in the lobby of our hotel with the rest of the group waiting for our bus to come. An older gentleman sits nearby and every time I turn his way, he's looking at me. It makes me feel so uneasy. I try to ignore it, shake it off, but I feel like he's undressing me with his eyes like I'm on display for him, and I hate it. My eyes start filling with tears.

"What's going on?" asks Helena as she rushes over seeing me upset.

"That man over there keeps staring at me. I feel like he's undressing me with his eyes," I tell her, feeling powerless like a complete victim.

"Maybe you remind him of his daughter or his wife or maybe he finds you beautiful," Helena says. I can tell she's annoyed by the wrinkled scowl on her face and is trying to offer me a different perspective. But I just can't shift gears in this moment.

As hard as I try, there is no way I'm going to experience this man any differently. The only thing I can do is to heal whatever is going on inside of me.

As we drive through the old city streets on the island of Crete, heading to Zeus' cave, I see sign after sign of "Aphrodite's Topless Girls" and "Aphrodite's Strip Club." I glance at the other members in our group, and no one seems to notice. I point them out to Lucia, the woman I'm sitting next to, and she casually rolls her eyes at the countless signs and chuckles. Apparently I'm alone with my feelings. Waves of rising anger mixed with tears of grief surface. *What have we done to the feminine? What have we done to sacred sexuality?* We haven't just suppressed the feminine, kept her quiet and hidden, we've turned her upside down. We've only allowed for the shadow side of the feminine to be revealed, and the shadow side of sex seems to be the only accessible side. I feel so incredibly degraded as a woman, seeing Aphrodite's name defamed.

I feel like a sacred sexual priestess returning to the temple lands after being gone for a couple thousand years and seeing everything that we worked so hard and so diligently to preserve and revere, in complete ruins. But it's more than being in ruins that strikes me, it's the rise of what takes its place. The display of women for the sole purpose of pleasing men. I know I've done this, and it makes me feel sick to my stomach. I see how women have clung to whatever power we can find during the reign of the patriarchy, and if it means that the only way to get a taste of our power is by dancing naked around a pole, shaking our breasts in front of a man's face and taking his money, then so be it. It doesn't take us to a place that we truly long for though, the sacred union, the freeing of the soul, the ecstatic dance between two lovers that sends us soaring into higher dimensions. My heart is both burning with rage and bleeding with deep sorrow.

I've always enjoyed sex and felt pretty free with my own sexuality as long as I'm in a committed relationship. But as I stand on sacred ground, where a culture of sacred sexual priestesses were once highly revered, I realize that my way of engaging in sex is actually a distraction, a protection of my inner child. It's a way for me to have a sense of power, but mostly, it's a way to hide my vulnerability.

Have I ever really felt safe with a man?

As our bus meanders through the city streets, making its way out to the rural areas of Crete, my thoughts wander to a WWII movie that I watched a few years back. A mother and her daughter are captured and questioned by two soldiers. When they threaten to harm her little girl, she steps forward. She seems like a very sweet, conservative woman, but in this moment, she reaches deep within herself pulling out the most reliable weapon she has for her and her little girl's survival — to become the archetypal whore. She offers herself to the soldiers in return for keeping her daughter safe. She knows the power she holds as a woman to create distraction, to prey on the only weakness the soldiers have and to give them something they won't pass up. Her eyes that previously shown nothing but fear, turn to a dark stare with an undeniable conviction and her posture changes from cowering to a pillar of strength. She surrenders to the power of the archetypal whore as she slowly unbuttons her simple, cotton dress from the neck down and pulls out the pin, freeing her long, dark hair from its tight bun. While holding the soldiers' attention with the power of her seduction as if casting a spell that leaves them powerless, she goes down on them, one soldier at a time as her little girl closes her eyes, burying her face in her hands. As I watched this scene, I remember saying out loud, "I would do that in a heartbeat to protect my child!"

As our bus enters the countryside of Crete, I realize the truth of this story. I've protected the sacredness of my Self, my own inner child, engaging in sex with the man I love in a way that keeps my most vulnerable self hidden, tucked away and safe.

The pattern to take care of my man and to serve him is deeply imbedded in my DNA. It's a real paradox. I have a potent memory of holding the power of being a sexual priestess and tried to become that for him, but I'm missing a huge piece. It's not about being comfortable and open and free to give him what he wants. It's about me and my most vulnerable self, teaching him how to approach me, how to touch me, how to read and respond to my body's most subtle clues to give me what I want and need so that I feel one hundred percent safe. The realization hits me hard, and I'm both excited that I found the magic key, but I also grieve. I see what I've done to myself all these years. My sacred whore took charge to protect the vulnerability of my sexual priestess that was left in the shadows, starving for a man's gentle touch, soft kisses and divine union.

Before heading to Zeus' cave, we stop at the archeological artifact museum in Heraklion. It's a small museum with statues of the Snake Goddess. She wears an intricately designed dress with a decorated apron and a bodice that reveals her voluptuous breasts and erect nipples. She wears a figure of a cat on the top of her head. In each hand, she holds a snake — a symbol of raising earth energy to meet cosmic energy. I've noticed this in almost every culture — images of gods and goddesses acting as the bridge between heaven and earth, the divine and the primal self in union. As I carefully study the Snake Goddess, my kundalini snake rouses at the base of my spine. I want to abandon all control and summon my snake power to rise, breaking any chains of fear and control, liberating me once and for all, but in the end, I walk away and join the rest of the group.

Getting back on our bus, we ride to Zeus' cave high up in the hills of Crete. Following a narrow footpath up the hill, I'm struck by the pungent aroma of rosemary and sage growing wild and the sweet smell of spring-blooming, pink anemones scattered throughout the landscape. It's a bouquet of savory and sweet fragrances that welcome me to the entrance of Zeus' cave. The contrast is poignant as I enter the cool, dank cave that smells of wet rock and decaying matter. Void of sunlight, I shuffle my feet across the well-worn dirt floor, lightly touching the wall of the cave and feeling the rough, moist stone. As our small group gathers in the center of the cave, my thoughts go to Maria Gimbutas' book, *The Language of the Goddess*, and I remember her saying, "Black does not mean death or the Underworld. It's the color of fertility, the color of damp caves and rich soil, of the womb of the Goddess where the life begins." It's the womb of the life-giving, regenerative power of the Dark Mother that I feel in this cave. There's an undeniable weight, like a magnet beneath the earth, pulling me in, a heaviness that leaves me questioning whether or not I'll be absorbed into the walls of the cave.

On a whim, I had brought my drum, Twin Moons with me to Greece and have carried it all the way up to the cave. As our group members find a place to sit and meditate, I stand near the small stream that meanders through the center of the cave and play my drum, singing back the life of the sexual priestess. As I play, my voice opens like a hollow channel with a song flowing out that feels like a healing river coming from below the earth. It feels like the Goddess herself. My left leg begins to tremble, so much so, I'm afraid I'm going to fall. The beat of the drum falls in sync with the heartbeat of the primordial mother and echoes throughout the earthen chamber. The sound lulls the women into a deep meditation, and they later share with me, that the cave and the beat of my drum was hypnotic as they entered into a trance-like state.

Feeling a bit wobbly, I sit down on the cold, dirt floor of the cave to rest. These are the words that come to me.

When you know you are safe, revered as a goddess and that your man has entered the garden gate in complete awe of you and with humility, then you will open up to new heights and bring your man with you. You're like a flower when the warm rays of the sun coax the bud open, petals falling to the side to capture the sun's rays, allowing the light to penetrate to its deepest core. It's all about you and your safety.

I take this potent message to heart. I see the healing that my sexual priestess needs. I no longer want to be in a position of serving or proving her power. I want to discover the joys of true partnership.

As I spend the next several days in Crete, visiting ancient ruins and walking to the shores of the Mediterranean, I ponder how I'm going to create change in my own relationship. It feels like a daunting task. So many patterns with the relationships in my life that I want to change feels like an immovable consciousness, a large fortress I have no idea how to penetrate. It's a mental construct designed to uphold the false belief that somehow men have more power. It's such a paradox because I feel the power of the feminine running through my blood and memories of thriving Goddess cultures woven in and out of my consciousness, but I can't escape the patriarchal construct that's so firmly in place, part of my own beliefs that are cemented into my psyche.

I entrust my healing to the continual ebb and flow of the Mediterranean hoping it will dissolve the old construct. It's a blessing to be immersed in the Minoan culture. They were a passionate people that revered ceremony and athletic games and beautiful art. When visiting the Knossos Temple, the center of the Minoan culture, I discover brightly painted walls, an alabaster throne and massive clay pots decorated with symbols. The interior walls display colorful images of people celebrating and dancing, animals and numerous dolphins leaping over images of spirals. Everywhere I look there are spirals painted on walls, carved into statues and engraved into jewelry. They radiate feminine energy, flowing, passionate and so healing.

As our time on the beautiful island of Crete is coming to an end, before flying to the nearby island of Cyprus, I offer my final handful of dried rose petals and sage to the waters on the shores of Crete thanking the land and the gods and goddesses for their healing and their tenderness.

After a short flight, we arrive in Cyprus, a small island in the Mediterranean just south of Turkey. Despite its size, it remains its own independent country. Turkey tried for many years to claim the island as their own but didn't succeed. There's a wall covered with photos of lost family members who disappeared during the Turkish military invasion of the northern one third of the island. The wall divides the Cyprus side of the island from the portion that Turkey claimed. The Cyprus side has been re-built after the war and is modern and sleek. I climb the tall, rickety steps to look over the other side of the wall to the Turkish side. It's bleak, nothing but the remains of destruction — void of life. In comparison to the side I stand on, it looks like a black and white photo. The destruction lays untouched, a place of desolation, while the other side is vibrant and alive. It reminds me of my time spent in the Underworld, my soul's desolate landscape. Now, I'm on the other side of the world on a beautiful Mediterranean island, with sunlit skies and tantalizing blue waters.

Our small bus makes its way through the city streets of Limassol and into the rural countryside of Cyprus to the Paphos area. Palaepaphos was once a major spiritual center back in 1200 BCE.

Our bus pulls off to the side of the road, and we follow a narrow footpath that goes under an old bridge where the road passes above. It's a stone tunnel that feels like a birth canal leading us to Aphrodite's birthplace. As we emerge out the other end, we are met by an old, crooked tree bent over the path with hundreds and hundreds of faded prayer ties. I reach in my bag, pulling out my scraps of fabric, say my prayers and tie them to the tree, joining the other prayers from all the pilgrims that walked this path before me.

Beyond the tree, the path leads us to a lovely, secluded beach on the shores of the Mediterranean. The sky is clear and the brilliant rays of the sun glisten on the calm waters. We take off our clothes, lay them on the warm, white sand and wade into the cool, turquoise water. The gentle waves rock me back and forth as I float, wishing my labors with my three children had been this gentle. I'm birthing myself, giving my body over to the sea goddess, surrendering to the beauty and letting go of my control and resistance, knowing I'm safe. I hear the whispers that I imagine come from the ancient priestesses that tended the temples, coaxing me to surrender, insuring me that my own birthing will be gentle and compassionate.

After floating in the cool birth waters, I wade out and onto the white, sandy beach. Finding a smooth rock, I lay down next to one of my traveling buddies, letting the sun dry and warm my chilled body. I feel more exposed than I'm comfortable with, despite the fact that all the other women in our small group are also resting, naked in the sun. There's one man in our group, and I observe myself as old and new patterns play themselves out in my mind. The old me would have convinced myself I didn't care about the man despite feeling uncomfortable around him. But the new me recognizes the need for discernment. My friend I lay next to, confirms my thoughts.

"I'm going to wear my towel because I'm not sure I want to expose myself in this way to his energy," she says, wisely before going over to where Helena and the man are sitting.

There have been so many times in my life where I had a tough attitude, *I can do what I want and that's their problem,* but I realize now this attitude hasn't really served me. Yes, it may be true that the place someone else is in may be their issue, but it's naive of me to believe that I won't be affected by someone else's energy. My friend's towel is a wise protection, a shield from any unwanted energy. A great lesson in personal boundaries and another step towards learning how to wisely cultivate safety for myself.

Nearby Aphrodite's birthplace is a temple dedicated to a goddess of fertility, most likely Aphrodite herself. There is no statue that's revered as in most temples, but instead a conical stone that the ancients worshiped. It doesn't consist of any familiar material known to this earth, a mystery that today remains unanswered. The stone now stands in a museum on the temple premises.

The dark gray stone stands alone. The only artifact in the small museum. It's about six feet tall, not like a huge standing stone, but pretty large. After everyone has a chance to visit the stone, I press my belly up against it and meditate. Within seconds, I see two large arms from inside the stone reach through with their hands and place five crystals inside my pelvis. *No wonder this stone was highly revered by the ancient ones.* I don't know what to think but feel humbled. A huge and welcomed gift has been bestowed on me. I don't experience any physical sensation. I carefully move away from the rock and look around the museum for the others. They had all ventured back outdoors visiting the temple grounds. Placing my hand over my pelvis, tears fill my eyes. This is the healing I was praying for, a womb cleansing. I believe this stone is made from a substance from another world and that it serves as a portal for beings to reach through from one dimension to another and offer healing. I wonder how many times people have passed by the powerful portal, seeing it as only a stone while before them stands this magnificent gateway to other dimensions.

I'm in disbelief, but excited like a child on Christmas morning. I don't mention it to anyone else in the group, but later that evening I go into Helena's room to visit. I ask her to "look" at me and see if she sees anything different. She tilts her head, like an old owl, as she peers into my energy field.

"Ahhh, you've had crystals placed in your pelvis, five of them."

"YES!"

This is such a great confirmation. Despite all the times I've had otherworldly experiences, I still look for confirmation.

The crystals inside me are like acupuncture needles, breaking up old and stuck energy and opening my meridians and healing my womb. My pelvis is tender for about two weeks, and I feel like I just had surgery.

We visit other temples dedicated to the sexual priestesses while in Cyprus. The story I feel at each temple is of battle-worn knights and kings coming to the temples and renewing their spirits through the art of sexual healing. I love this idea as a powerful way to support the warriors who are plagued with scars on their soul from the horrors of war. I imagine a warrior, burdened with grief after taking lives of others — fathers, brothers and sons, coming to the temple with great reverence for the Goddess. He'd be taken to the baths and then gently caressed with fragrant oils and healing balms before entering the priestess' chamber. As she made love to him, she would hold in her heart his god-self as the power of the Goddess entered her and mended his broken spirit. This is so needed today as we witness the suffering of our warriors who return home unable to release the trauma of war and remain broken and in anguish.

My trip to Greece and to Cyprus is coming to an end. And while I still pray every day, making my offering to the gods and goddesses, I don't feel I've completed my work. I'm so incredibly grateful for having received many beautiful gifts here, but am still longing for union with my dark haired "sister." *Didn't I pray hard enough? Was my intuition wrong?* I go to bed heavy hearted as though I had failed my mission. I eventually fall asleep feeling that I somehow let myself down and had flown all the way over here, leaving my children and Ricardo without completing my task at hand. I know I'm being pretty hard on myself, but the feeling nags at me. Eventually I fall asleep but am awakened hours later.

I'm down to the final hour of my sacred journey. The goddess does not fail me. I wake in the middle of the night, just an hour before I'm to get up and leave for my early flight home. Standing before me, in the space of a thin veil, is my "sister" with the long dark hair, and with her, a beautiful, blond-haired little girl. My heart breaks wide open as I receive them in with such joy and gratitude, tears streaming down my cheeks. It's a union that I feel I've been waiting for for a couple thousand years. I'll never completely understand what this moment is for me. Is this a part of myself from another lifetime? I really don't know. All I know is, I've been searching for them for a very long time, turning myself inside out, traversing the most difficult of inner landscapes and here they are, on the shores of the Mediterranean, coming through the mist that veils the other worlds, called by my many, many prayers. I felt so broken, and now, so filled with joy. *Thank you, thank you, dear Goddess. I will forever serve you.*

Saying goodbye to Helena as I leave for my early flight home, she looks at me with her twinkling eyes and says, "I see you got what you came looking for."

"Thank you, I love you," I whisper in her ear as I hug her goodbye.

Chapter 13

Resurrecting
the Dragon

I pull you out of the depths of where you've been banished, cutting through the entangled vines and thick roots that have kept you in the dark, hiding, locked away, chained to the walls of the old, stone dungeon. With my sword of truth in hand, I cut away the gnarled entrance and slash your shackles, freeing you, pulling you up and out into the bright shining light of day. Here, you will rest with the flowers, smell the fresh green grass, spread your wings and fly, and let out your mighty breath of fire.

"I don't want it in my house," I say to Ricardo, with a mix of tears and anger.

"It's no big deal!" he says, defensively.

"Well, it is to me. It goes against everything I'm trying to cultivate.

As another summer camp season comes to an end, Ricardo spends more and more time in our spare room that we converted into an office. After putting the kids to bed one evening, I walk in to talk with him and find him looking at pornography. I struggle with this so much because on one hand, I feel as a "modern-day" woman, I'm not supposed to have a problem with pornography — I should rise above it or embrace it. BUT I CAN'T. It puts me right back on the bus in Greece and seeing all the Aphrodite topless dance clubs. And I'm angry, not just with Ricardo, but the state of our world. I'm angry with all the temptations — so many seductive, yet empty promises where people get swallowed up in the clutches of darkness. And yet, I know how important it is for me to know darkness and to learn from it.

Over the next few days, as my anger gnaws at me, I know there's something more for me to see and learn. But I'm tired. One initiation after another with no time in between for a "regular" life.

"Do you have to dig into everything? Can't you just take a break and be okay with the way things are?" asks Ricardo, frustrated with my continual inner work.

"Well, I'd like to, but I'm not okay with the way things are. And yeah, I'm exhausted and frustrated with it, too," I respond.

I'm not experiencing the joy I felt my last night in Greece. I'm now painfully aware of a sinister voice inside my head and a sneering, grimacing face of a man that pops into my dreams at night. The only person in my life that rouses the same feelings is my ex-husband. *Are they one and the same?* Moments of fear ripple through my body when he threatens to take the children or take away the child support. He desperately wants to have control over me, and his attempt, however futile, always coincides when my power is growing.

I completely understand what Ricardo is talking about in regards to taking a rest. But how can I? I'm confronted with one thing after another that I just can't turn away from.

Days later, our realtor calls. She found a buyer for our house. We plan on finding a place to rent while we build our new home on our new land. My attention fully turns towards packing and cleaning, and for awhile, it's a welcome break from the incessant voice in my head.

The only available home we find to rent is an old, historic stone house in town. It's quite large, with many rooms, and just a block away from the lake.

"I'm not sure we can afford this house," Ricardo whispers, leaning away from the realtor.

"Well, let's just see," I say, as I continue browsing the downstairs.

I step out onto the front porch facing the nearby lake. I visited this lake when I was a teenager many times. It was my go-to place for healing my broken heart, finding answers to my teenage dilemmas and connecting with a deeper part of myself. A large willow tree stands at its edge. I call her "Grandmother Willow." Far down the east side of the lake is an old stone tower that juts from the shores. A plaque from the late 1800's reads, "King Fisher Tower, dedicated to the Lady of the Lake." It's the Lady of the Lake that I summoned as a young girl, and swore I saw her rise out of the center of the lake, gliding across the water towards me. Even then, I unknowingly beseeched the Divine Feminine in times of need. And now, she's summoning me. Like a gentle breeze coming from the lake, she reaches out to me as I once had to her.

"It'll work out," I whisper to Ricardo. "This is where we need to be right now," I tell him with utter confidence.

After moving in, I find the house is even more perfect than I had first realized. Every evening as the sun begins to set, hundreds of bats fly out of the eves from the attic, making their way around town and to the lake to feast on bugs. Between the energy of the bats and the old stone walls, I have my own cave, and it feels perfect to complete the type of work I'm doing.

After a couple of months of getting settled into our temporary home, I travel with Kelly to Pennsylvania to participate in a healing sweat lodge for women with a Lakota medicine woman. It's three lodges, spread out over three days. We stay in a tepee in her backyard, close to the sweat lodge area. Our weekend begins early in the morning as the sun is just coming up over the horizon. There are four other women besides Kelly and myself, and we spend a good hour searching for large rocks and firewood. The medicine woman, Dorothy, is a tall, older woman, who teaches us exactly what type of rocks to choose and exactly how to build the fire to heat them with very precise directions. I can tell she's done this many, many times. I make a small tinder bundle out of dried grasses and birch bark to hold the spark and with one blow, it bursts into flames. The dry firewood catches quickly and soon, flames engulf the rocks. When they begin to glow orange and red from the intense heat, we know it's time to change into our ceremonial dresses.

Barefoot, I crawl on my hands and knees with several other women across the damp, dirt threshold into the dark lodge to find a place to sit. The lodge is void of any light, no cracks revealing the sunlit day or pinholes to remind us of the light. I can't see my own hand held in front of my face. The darkness of the womb.

One by one, the woman who tends the fire passes hot rocks into the lodge with a shovel until the pit is full. Using a wooden ladle, Dorothy chants in a deep, throaty voice as she pours water from a bucket over the rocks which hiss and spit, generating intense steam. By the time all the hot rocks are added to the pit, we shift as far as we can to the outer walls of the lodge, lying down close to the cool earth while covering our faces with towels to protect our skin. The smell of cedar and sage and copal waft through the heavy, steam-filled air, and I sink deeply into my roots and into the womb of mother earth. I hate the heat and have no choice but to surrender.

In between songs and chants, Dorothy works with each of us individually. She's a Lakota shaman, and she dispels demons. My eyes never adjust to the darkness, but as I listen to her work with each woman, my thoughts return to Inanna's descent. At the end of the story, Sylvia Pererra describes the demons that Inanna encounters in the Underworld. She embraces and befriends them, and they become her most powerful allies. That always felt right to me. I'm having a hard time connecting to Dorothy's work.

The lodge lasts for four long, grueling hours and we all crawl out, hot, sweaty and tired. The crisp, fall air is a welcome relief. We shower and gather in her home for a meal. Minutes after exiting the lodge, waves of nausea rise, and I spend the rest of the evening bent over the toilet, throwing up while listening to the clinking of forks and plates and women chattering. No one quite knows what is going on with me, and I see the concerned looks from the other women and especially from Dorothy. I'm not sure what's going on either but sense it has to do with the way Dorothy works. Ever since I was little, whenever I swallowed someones else's fear, I'd vomit it out like it was poisoned food. It started in kindergarten with a teacher that ruled her class of five year olds like a drill sergeant. I vomited every morning before school.

I wake the next morning feeling a bit better, but low on energy. Again, we gather rocks and firewood, then crawl back into the lodge. When it comes to my turn, Dorothy "casts out a demon" and chants as she's done with everyone else. As she continues her chanting, her voice grows more and more intense. The other women are now chanting with her, their voices growing louder and louder. Everything becomes heightened, and I sense fear in her voice.

"Tell it to go, tell it to go!" she yells frantically. Her now shrill voice doesn't match her usual calm, grounded demeanor.

This feels so wrong. I don't know why. I'm so confused. She's yelling at me with apparent distress, and the women's chanting continues to grow louder. So, I do what she says not knowing who or what I'm telling to leave.

I shout, "Go! Leave!"

But as soon as I do what she's asked, I hear the familiar "who cooks for you" hoot of an owl in a tree right next to the lodge. It starts hooting incessantly in the middle of the day. An unusual time for owls to be flying around, and definitely not the softer cooing of a mourning dove that is often mistaken for an owl.

As the other women comment on the oddity of the owl's hooting, I know in my gut this is a message for me. I immediately think of my animal medicine cards and remember the message of the owl.

Betrayal!

It's a warning! I've just betrayed myself, and once again, I crawl out of the lodge on my hands and knees and spend the next few hours bent over a toilet. I retreat to the tepee early and curl up in my sleeping bag near a small fire. It's a cold, fall night in November, and I so much want to be back home in my warm bed.

I wake early in the morning and get a fire going in the tepee to warm my frozen toes and fingers. As I lie on my sleeping bag, stoking the fire, my thoughts wander to yesterday's lodge. There's something I'm missing. It's not the pleasurable healing experience I'm hoping for, but instead, a lesson to be learned. I imagined feeling good, feeling cleansed, feeling energized after each lodge, but the opposite has been true.

It's our final lodge, and I crawl in with trepidation, but with my eyes wide open. I'm determined to figure this out. I'm going to stand in my truth no matter what.

The lodge is long. We've been in for hours, and my skin feels dangerously hot. As Dorothy works with the other women, I lie on the dirt floor of the lodge, as far away from the fire as I can and cover my face with a towel. The air is dense and heavy with hot steam. Any cool air I can find coming in through the bottom of the lodge is a welcome relief. When it's my turn, I sit up, where the air is hotter and feel dizzy. She begins her chanting, and the same thing happens.

"Tell it to go! Trista, you have to tell it to go!" she yells, frantically.

And again, the women's chanting grows louder as before.

I saw this moment coming. I played it over and over again in my mind earlier in the morning. I'm prepared.

"No. It doesn't feel right to me. I won't do it," I say.

"What are you talking about? You have to do this," she says, her voice shrill.

"No, I don't. Whatever it is you see that you are calling a demon is a part of me, and I won't tell it to go. I need to transmute this," I say confidently.

My words and calm demeanor are a sharp contrast to her demands and the heightened energy inside the lodge.

She starts to argue with me, but quickly retreats. There's a wave of uneasiness that ripples through the lodge. For a moment, I'm not sure how this is going to play out. *Is she furious with my questioning her? Am I banished from the lodge? Are all the women going to shun me?* With bated breath, I wait, unable to see her expression in the darkness. A moment in time that feels a thousand times longer, but in reality, only a few seconds.

"What are you feeling?" she asks, her disposition now calm and relaxed.

The other women exhale, with apparent relief by Dorothy's response.

"I believe what you're seeing is a part of me that I've demonized because I've been afraid of it," I respond. "I need to heal this myself." And as I speak, I feel a crystal pillar rise up through my core from the earth. I feel its well-defined edges, but also its brilliant light. The female phallus that rises up from the womb of the earth in moments of great truth. I am the light filled chalice.

I feel Dorothy's warm hand squeeze my arm with what I think is an agreement. For the first time, I crawl out of the lodge feeling energized rather than nauseous. The other women comment on how incredible I look, seeing a light in my eyes they hadn't seen before.

As we all meet in the house for our final potluck, I notice Dorothy has a hard time looking at me. Eventually, she pulls me aside.

"You shouldn't do this work by yourself," she says, in a scolding voice. "It's dangerous!" she adds.

"I'm not afraid. I know what I'm doing," I say as I give her a hug goodbye.

I'm relieved to get back home. It was a long and tiresome weekend. The next day, I set up a small table in front of our bedroom window that faces the lake and cover it with a delicate, red silk scarf, a beeswax candle and the snake goddess statue I brought back from Crete. This is my altar, my focal point for healing my "demon." The voice in my head grows worse the closer I get to transmuting it.

I hear the contemptuous voice telling me I'm a whore, telling me I'm ugly, telling me I'm a slut. All through the day, every day. And every time I hear the voice, I go to my altar to re-program the messages.

Kneeling in front of my altar, I light the candle, and watch shadows dance across the face of the snake goddess. I look in the direction of the lake and feel its loving energy.

"I am beautiful. I am powerful. I am sacred," I repeat over and over again.

The voice gets louder and more gripping. Each time, I stop in the middle of whatever I'm doing and go to my altar. Even when Jessi has a friend over to play. I go to my altar and kneel before it. This time with my daughter on one side and her friend Abby on the other side. *This feels so right — teaching them to pray to the goddess.* We sit in silence for a bit and then sing a song, just the three of us.

One day, while Matthew and Jessi are in school, Javi is at my parents' house and Ricardo is working on building our new home, I decide to dance with my "demon." I put on some music and wrap a ceremonial scarf around my waist, light candles and invite the demon to dance. I move my hips back and forth, swaying to the haunting music, enticing the demon to join me. In my mind's eye, I see it trying to hide from the light, but I continue moving to the music and summoning the demon. I feel calm and confident, void of fear. The power has shifted. It no longer has power over me, instead, I'm the one wielding the power. I sing with the music and the energy in the room becomes dense, heavy and formidable. Time stands still. I feel my roots deepen into the mysteries of the earth. I see it standing before me — ugly and red-eyed. But still, I'm not afraid.

This must have been what the medicine woman saw and why she was so afraid.

I remember my experience at the Long Meg stone circle in England and know I need to embrace it and give it my love.

I imagine the demon as an infant as I continue to dance. Infants, no matter what kind of being, are in their purest form and so easy to love. So, I dance with my demon, visualizing it as an innocent infant, and its ugliness begins to melt away, changing into a magnificent, green dragon. She's shy, but powerful. I have so much compassion and joy for the dragon that timidly stands in front of me. She's beautiful. I realize that my demons are all of my own creation.

Somewhere along the way, I had received the message this part of me was bad, not good, dangerous, shameful, something to fear, and I had believed it. Perhaps it's from this lifetime, or perhaps my dragon had been banished to the Underworld when the old ways were overshadowed by the new, incoming Christian religion a thousand and more years ago. The once revered serpent energy, turned evil. I'm so happy and in awe of my dragon.

Later that night, feeling content with my day's work, I fall into a deep sleep and have a dream.

I am in Helena's healing room in the basement of her house. I lie on her massage table and see her backyard as I look through the large sliding glass doors to my right. Helena is talking to me as she stands at my feet. I lift my head to see what she's doing. Looking down at my feet, I see the enormous legs of a dragon. I reach down and stroke the iridescent green scales as I run my hands down my large, strong dragon legs. Helena looks up at me. "Your tail is especially beautiful," she comments as she runs her hand gently down my long tail.

I wake the next morning feeling incredibly renewed. My mind is free from voices. I 'm super excited to get to know my dragon. While some cultures depict dragons as evil beasts that a hero needs to slay, to me, dragons are powerful and magical beings. They represent earth consciousness, the realm of the Goddess. And unlike my test of will, courage and strength that gave me the sword, the years spent surrendering to deep emotions, unraveling wrongful myths and beliefs, has been a process of self-emptying. Now, I am no longer bound by societal expectations and familial beliefs, but instead, deeply rooted in the earth. I am the cauldron.

Our time in the stone house comes to an end as our new, cottage-like home at Hawk Circle is complete. I walk down to the lake with a handful of dried rose petals and sage.

"Thank you, dear Lady of the Lake. Thank you for always helping me to heal."

I toss my offering, and the wind carries it out into the lake scattering it across the glass-like surface.

The Sacred Marriage
The Path of Union

*The Sacred Marriage is the union between two polar opposites.
It is the oneness found within duality. The Sacred Marriage
is meant to hold, contain and unify that which appears
to be opposite. When the two come together, it creates a third,
and that third is the Divine.*

*In Celtic mythology, it is represented by the Cup and the Sword
coming together. Or often, it is an image of a man and a woman
with the dove appearing above them. The dove is the divine spirit
that enters the space of equilibrium held between the two pillars.*

*What appears to be separate is all but an illusion. The boundaries
that we create in our minds dissolve if we are open to the other,
open to the possibility, the potential. In our openness of both
heart and mind, grace enters and there is the
marriage - the essence of the divine.*

*It's the serpent that meets the dove. The dragon that becomes
the winged horse. Or the man and the woman that creates
the Divine child.*

Chapter 14
Void of Soul,
Infused with Fear

I *remember entering this world, as a tiny newborn, pulled from my mother's womb with ice-cold forceps, blinding fluorescent lights and the strong hands of the doctor that held me upside down and gave me a spank. Where was the warmth, the gentle flow that I was used to as I was rocked in my mother's amniotic fluid for months? I'm shocked to return to the earth I love and spend the rest of my life searching for the feminine. Where did she go? Where is she hiding? Why is this world so void of soul? I call to her, "Sophia, Magdalena, Dark Mother?" but ultimately know I must first awaken her within my own heart and womb where she lays sleeping.*

Moving into our new home is exciting, and it's a relief to be living on our magical land. Our house is situated at the base of the hill next to a nearby pond, not too far from the old farmhouse where our wilderness instructors live. We can see the valley and the rolling, green hills across the way from our living room and bedroom windows. Javi has a cute room just off the kitchen, easy for him to get in and out of with his new little wheelchair. Matthew and Jessi have the whole upstairs for their bedrooms and a loft for playing. We're surrounded by woods, and every evening I hear the wild call of coyotes running in the field behind our home. In the mornings, I wake seeing deer just a few yards from our bedroom window.

I start working with some of our young female staff and apprentices that join us for the summer. We crawl into our teepee that Ricardo and I set up in the field, light a small fire, sing songs, and sip herbal tea as I share stories of female heroins' trials and tribulations on the path to finding their power. The young women drink in the stories and the imagery, longing to express their feminine power and understand their intuition. On a few occasions, I need to redirect their thinking.

"I think we're so much smarter than men. They just don't get some of the most basic principles to having a relationship," complains Nellie as she rolls her eyes in exasperation. Nellie, along with most of the women in the tepee are young, some still teenagers.

"This is not what our lodge is about," I respond firmly. "You do not find your power as a woman by putting a man down. That is not true power. This is a path that's about YOU and how you respond to life," I say clearly.

"But that's what the men have done, haven't they?" Responded Emma, one of our apprentices. "They've put women down for hundreds of years as they grew in power."

"Yes, but look where it's gotten them. An out of balance world, no true partnership and an unfulfilled longing that will never be satisfied," I respond. "We are the remedy. Growing in power isn't about getting back at the men. It' about creating a new world," I respond passionately.

We create a beautiful, inspiring and healing space at Hawk Circle, but we long to share this with the men. It's just not the right time. With the enthusiastic help from our female staff and apprentices, I create a safe space for us to explore our feminine power and to enter into both the sacred womb and the inner most sanctuary of our heart. To invite the men into the space wasn't appropriate. Like the temples I visited, there are many doorways, each leading one right after the other to the furthest back room, the sacred, inner sanctuary. Very few enter this space except for the high priestesses. The tepee is our sacred sanctuary.

One evening after hearing our songs and our outrageous laughter spilling out of the tepee all the way down the hill to the front porch of the farmhouse, the young men approach us and ask us what it is we do in our lodges. They want to create a similar experience. I gladly share the information with them, but they struggle to create a lodge for themselves, never finding the time. Though it pains us women to see this, we know this is a path that only they can walk.

In the privacy of late night gatherings in the tepee, nestled together and sharing our stories, our feminine power grows. It's powerful, and we intuitively remember what it's like when women lived together creating a life that honored the goddess. But outside the tepee, we're met with the rigidity of the patriarchal mindset. There's the constant drive to work. Whether it's weeding in the garden or working on building projects, it's all approached with a relentless thrust, leaving no time for contemplation, or fun or for just being. My heart breaks. This isn't the vision I imagined creating with Ricardo.

When I first met him, he lived his life on his own terms, running a wilderness camp for kids. But now, after buying this land with the intent of growing Hawk Circle, I feel like I just stepped back into the 1950's and the only value I have is taking care of the children and making sure dinner is on the table. The stress of trying to grow Hawk Circle and raise a child with special needs weighs heavy on Ricardo. At least this is my guess. When I ask him what he's feeling, it's like poking a wasp nest. He explodes with countless excuses as to why he has no choice but to continue working hard with little time to consider any other solutions. I'm crushed. I feel bruised by his rigid and harsh mindset. When we go for walks, I hope for heartfelt moments as we explore our woods together, but instead I'm met with lists of what needs to be done coupled with far-fetched dreams of our place that continue to dangle just out of reach.

"We can't create outside what we have yet to create within," I say to Ricardo as we head home from a morning walk to the stream.

"You keep saying that, but I don't get what you mean," he responds sincerely, yet with an edge of frustration.

"Well, the way we experience life, every situation is a direct reflection of what's inside us, our inner landscape. If we haven't cultivated the feeling or the space for abundance within us, then we can't create it outside of ourselves," I say.

"I don't know if that's true. I think if you work hard enough, then you get results," he says with a hint of exasperation.

"When it isn't cultivated within, then our unconscious patterns literally block our ability to receive," I respond, with growing irritation.

We have many conversations of this nature, and they rarely bring us closer to a shared understanding. But I also ask myself, "Why am I having this experience? If my outer world experience is a reflection of my inner world, then why am I having this experience with Ricardo?"

Deeply sad, I retreat to my inner world, continually asking myself how to shift this. The only answer that comes to me is to continue standing in my truth and to let the feelings come and wash through me. My path is to hold the power of the feminine and to lead from this place, but it's hard and so disheartening. It's not a way of leading that anyone recognizes — void of a hierarchical order. I feel so invisible. I continually surrender to my feelings and often retreat to heal my wounds. I imagine my experience to be similar to the long, generational line of women that came before me living in a world with no room for the feminine, devalued and ignored until they quietly fade into the shadows. Only I refuse to fade away, so I fight trying anything I can to carve out a space for myself like a wild animal baring its teeth at its captor.

I'm trying to resurrect the temples of the Divine feminine, but instead I'm experiencing the same oppressive energy that's responsible for their downfall. I'm confronted with my own ruins only they aren't ancient, they're here in present time, and staring me in the face every day.

One day, while at a board meeting for Hawk Circle, I suggest we slow down and take some time to feel out what our strategy for moving forward should be.

"I think it would be a good idea for us to take some time to contemplate and tune into the best way for us to move forward," I suggest. The board looks at me as though I'm crazy.

"Well what else is there to know? We have to advertise," responds Bill, an older man who's had many years of business experience.

"We don't really have time to just meditate on this. We have to implement a plan and keep moving forward," says Ricardo, obviously frustrated.

"But we continue to encounter struggle. So, I don't believe this is an issue that can solely be resolved by yet another marketing strategy. I'm suggesting that as a group, we practice listening or meditating, with the understanding that we're collaborating with spirit and allowing our vision to have a life of its own," I say, on the brink of losing my patience.

In my mind, I lunge forward, throwing a dagger and sticking it into the center of their meeting table. And with one swift motion erase their strategy written on a white board and replace it with an image of the Hindu goddess, Kali—wild-haired, tongue hanging out, a skull in one hand and a blade in the other. No words spoken, just swift action that says, "This is the end of patriarchal rule!" But instead, I'm silent with clenched teeth.

On one occasion, I do snap at the president of our board who's wanting to implement a very aggressive sales strategy. He gets so offended by my candid response, that he gets up and leaves, for good.

I'm disappointed and furious with being so disregarded. They're all on a fast moving train, full steam ahead, with no introspection, no listening and no collaboration. This scenario repeats countless times during other board meetings.

My words fall on deaf years, as the small group of board members continues with their planning and strategizing. I come from such a different mindset than everyone else sitting at the table and have no idea as to how to share my world with them. This vision that stirred inside of me years ago when I first returned home from Peru, before I even met Ricardo, speaks of something different, and I struggle to find the words. I feel its essence, like how I imagine the temples and the goddess worshipping cultures to be during the height of their existence, people working together in alignment with a higher purpose, collaborating with both the seen and unseen forces of nature, celebrations of life, time spent in prayer and ceremony. Balance, maybe that's the main difference.

I have flashbacks of past lives where I stand at a sacred temple as it falls into the hands of the intruder, desperately trying to save what's being taken from me. I also have flashbacks of my life as a little girl when I begin noticing that my dad has the last say in everything as though his voice and his opinion is what matters far beyond mine and the rest of the family's. I feel so lost at times with no road map and pray every night for answers.

It's particularly hard for me when Matthew watches this dynamic play out between Ricardo and myself. He was born with the bright blue eyes of consciousness. He looks at me with a penetrating and all-knowing gaze. He says nothing, but he doesn't have to. His eyes say it all. I'm crippled with shame, wanting to be stronger and better for him, for all my children, but most of the time, I'm stricken with grief and rage.

I know you see the truth of this, sweetie. I know you see what is going on. Are you wondering why I'm putting up with this? Do you think less of me? I know my actions remain invisible. Please trust me. It matters to me what you think, but I need to follow my inner guidance on this one.

I'm not experiencing this just with the Hawk Circle board and Ricardo, although this is so close to my heart, it's where it hurts the most. I experience this at my children's school. I make frequent visits there suggesting other ways to work with the children that empower them rather than shame them and allow room for the child's own innate wisdom to unfold. Again, I'm met with blank stares or a shake of the head. When Javi has one of his hospital stays, which fortunately are becoming less and less frequent, I sit in the hospital for hours on end as he sleeps, thinking how to create a space that would be more conducive to healing, offering healthy meals and a more welcoming environment. Everywhere I look, I see a world that lacks the feminine aspect and little to stir the soul awake. While I'm deeply sad, I'm also determined to never give up.

Hope is the light we hold onto during dark times, and I'm holding on for dear life. Without hope, I'd have nothing. It's the only thread that holds together the prospect of change.

Raised to do well in school, go to college and have a career, my parents taught me how to succeed in the patriarchal world. But this is different. I'm bringing in the voice of the feminine, the balancing force to the masculine, trying to create change while hitting one brick wall after another, getting knocked down and getting back up again and again. Whenever I take it personally, which is frequently, I hear the message whispered in my ear, "This isn't all about you. You're doing the work of the priestess." At times, I get back up and straighten my crown when hearing this message. Other times, fold my arms across my chest and stomp my feet declaring my resignation.

One morning, I wake early and head out for a walk before the rest of my family wakes up. A heavy mist settles in the valley giving the illusion that the rolling hills are now tall mountains. This is my absolute favorite experience living here — the morning mist is a regular occurrence, and I love how it changes the landscape as it dances through the valley. I walk up the trail behind our house feeling the stones pull me towards them. I head into the woods, pausing to take in the beauty. Slender birch trees stand tall like faerie queens and kings perfectly positioned in and around the large boulders. This is our stone circle, brought here by glaciers so very long ago.

I mindfully place a slice of homemade bread on the altar stone and douse it with herbal infused wine I made last winter.

"This is my offering to you. Thank you for watching over our land and the people who come here." A slight breeze caresses my face, and I know it's their acknowledgment of my offering.

I go to one of the largest stones in the circle and lean against it, closing my eyes to connect with the inner plane of our land. The birds' singing becomes hushed as I slip into a meditative state. Here, I see a small gathering of Native Americans in council, and other beings, faeries from the Otherworld. They appear from behind the silvery bark of the birch trees. One of them motions to me. I follow along a path that wanders through large oaks and ends at the brink of a hill overlooking an expansive vista.

The view is breathtaking, like seeing the entire earth. The landscape sparkles and shines with an emerald green glow. Everything feels so alive and vibrant. But just as I inhale its beauty, dark, stormy clouds roll in, and the once shining landscape turns into a dark and crumbling world. I see fighting and discord and feel a tremendous amount of fear and anger from the people. It's so unsettling and breaks my heart seeing such a stark contrast between the potential of a world of abundance, and the crumbling that feels inevitable.

The energy shifts, and despite the horrible scene playing out in front of me, I feel a tremendous amount of peace. Three, faceless beings of light appear before me assuring me that all will be okay, and my family and I will always be safe here. The crumbling world feels necessary so the new can be ushered in. And within seconds, I'm back leaning against the stone in our own woods.

The sun is now fully over the hill, and I know my family is probably up by now, so I head back down the trail. I see clearly how my experiences with the old forms of power are providing me with the skills to help build the new out of the rubble. I know I need to understand true power. A power that empowers people, strengthens communities, dispels fear and creates world-wide peace and unity. This is not something that can be taught nor understood intellectually. I need to dismantle my own personal patriarchal construct so I can disentangle myself from the threads of fear that hold the old paradigm together.

Moments later, I stand in the kitchen mixing batter for zucchini muffins. The children are quietly chatting with one another on the couch, and Ricardo is heading out to mow the lawn. Stirring the batter, I feel like the primordial mother stirring her cauldron, and it brings me into a trance. I see I'm part of a soul group of women that are doing the underground work to dismantle the patriarchal construct to make way for the feminine. But still, I feel so alone.

I imagine myself as one of the priestesses from the ancient temples, returning to this world, working my magic even as the others, spread wide across the world with oceans between us, do their magic. I imagine each of them wondering, as do I, where the others are, wishing we were all together. But instead, we're spread out through the world with our own separate cauldrons, and our own private stirring a new world into being.

Late September, well after school starts and the kids are settled in, I make plans to join Helena on a trip to Turkey, Anatolia, one of the oldest civilizations in the world. While it has only been a year and a half since my trip to Greece, the sacred marriage aspect of the journey to Turkey is calling me. Helena reached out earlier in the spring. She knew the extent of what I had been working through and offered me a partial scholarship for her trip to Turkey. I was so grateful to have her looking out for me. She knew we were tight on money because of our move. Her offer was such a welcomed surprise.

As I pack my bags for my next trip, I also "pack" my grief to carry and handover to the ancient mother lands of Turkey.

Chapter 15

Turkey and the Primordial Mother

The ancient mother goddess calls to me deep from the cradle of civilization. Humming her tune with primordial chords, unexplained feelings from deep in my belly begin to stir. From far away lands, over mountains and across oceans, I hear her tune travel through time like the morning mist across the sea. My soul awakens and takes the helm, steering me back to her.

Sitting in the square of Old Istanbul, I watch the Turkish people communing with one another, taking a break from their day and enjoying each other's company. The nearby restaurant has large, wooden tables scattered about the old city square, with tarnished copper hookahs stationed at each table. I notice only men sitting around the tables, enjoying a drink and smoke, except for maybe a small handful of tourists.

"We don't see this in the U.S. Even when people are taking a break in the middle of their day, there's still a sense of rushing," I say to one of my travel companions.

"So true!" she responds.

The apple tea tastes yummy and sweet, and I inhale the bright colors of reds and oranges and blues that are such a part of the vibrant landscape of the Turkish people. The colors are woven into their rugs, their tapestries and the old worn cushion I'm sitting on.

The music playing in the square has a beautiful haunting quality to it, and I make a connection to the music I danced to with my dragon the winter before. It has the same earthy sensuality to it, and I remember reading that the artist's music had been inspired by her years of living in Turkey.

The music continues and three Whirling Dervishes come to dance dressed in long, white tunics with black sashes, and small red, conical caps. I study their feet, wearing worn, black, ballet-type slippers, taking small steps as they begin to spin. The stark white "skirts" extend out like large, flowing rotating disks as they spin faster and faster, their arms gracefully lifting from their sides as they move the energy from the earthly plane high into the heavens. I'm completely mesmerized watching the Dervishes twirl to the haunting music. They are the semazens or whirlers that belong to the Mevlevi sect of the Sufi, an Islamic practice to achieve divine knowledge. Their dance is an active meditation that represents the earth spinning on its axis as it revolves around the sun.

This is the dance with my dragon. When I freed it from its chains, danced the spiral dance until it took flight and soared to the heavens.

We stay only two nights in old Istanbul, giving us just enough time to visit the beautiful Hagia Sophia, also known as The Church of Divine Wisdom, and the famous Blue Mosque.

"The Hagia Sophia, a cathedral built in the 6th century and now a museum, is considered one of the greatest buildings of the world, once the largest cathedral ever built, and the only cathedral to house three different religions, Pagan, Christian Orthodox and Sunni Islam," explains our Turkish guide, Ahmed.

I'm humbled, standing outside its impressive entrance.

"Opposite the Hagia Sophia is the Blue Mosque, built centuries later by Sultan Ahmet when he was only twelve years old. It's a purely Muslim structure, different from the mixed heritage of the Hagia Sophia. It's still active for daily prayer, and at other times, open for tourists," says Ahmed, brushing his thick, dark hair from his eyes. He speaks with such a deep, accented voice, his words gracefully rolling off his tongue, and his dark skin contrasted by his stark white tunic. As he looks my way and his warm, brown eyes meet mine, I quickly turn away fearing he'll pick up on my thoughts that are far from the history of Hagia Sophia.

We visit during daily prayer. Wrapping my head with a scarf so only my eyes are showing, as is the custom, I enter the mosque with the rest of our group finding a place in the back to sit and pray. I'm amazed at its size, later discovering that it can hold 10,000 people during prayer. The entire inside is covered with intricately, hand-painted blue tiles, from floor to all the way across the ceiling. I can't imagine the labor that went into tiling the immense structure. Ricardo and I had spent hours tiling our small bathroom with a mixture of Italian and Mexican tiles.

Like my first trip to Chartres Cathedral in France, I observe the Turkish women's daily ritual of attending prayer, sitting comfortable on cushions, most wearing black robes from head to foot. Their dark eyes reveal nothing, neither friendliness nor annoyance, only ambivalence. Again, I'm curious as to what they are praying for? This is such a different culture than France. The women appear to be dedicated to the daily prayer as I observe them entering the mosque, comfortably settling in as though returning to their same seat each day. I'm instantly aware that I'm possibly taking one of their seats and am prepared to give up my cushion if I sense this to be true. Their dedication feels different, more habitual than the fervent praying by the old, French women who appeared to be deeply devoted to the Black Madonna. The contrast is similar to the times in my life when I perform daily rituals until they become a natural part of my day, as opposed to other times where I'm bent over in prayer, requesting help, healing and change. The first feels more like maintenance.

Leaving Ahmed and Istanbul, our bus makes its way through the cradle of civilization, following the Silk Road, the ancient caravan route that links central China to the eastern Mediterranean. We pass several small towns, winding our way through hills and valleys. Most of the homes in the countryside are small and surrounded by collard greens and squash plants that trail endlessly down the hillsides. There's an endearing quality to the people's simple lifestyle and I wonder how I can incorporate what I'm seeing at Hawk Circle. It looks much easier to have food growing all over the place rather than in a contained garden that needs constant tending. It's untamed, free to grow wherever it wants, requiring little effort from the cultivator. Working with the board and growing Hawk Circle feels unnecessarily difficult and restrictive. I'm craving a more natural, wild and organic way.

As we arrive in southern Anatolia, we visit Catalhoyuk where ruins of the goddess culture existed as early as 7500BCE. Signs of the ancient people being the first agriculture communities to exist on earth, growing grain in the fertile crescent and raising domesticated farm animals, leaves a tangible impression. I hadn't thought of people this far back in history, being so advanced in their means of creating an agrarian culture, but as it was being excavated in the 1950's, they found old grain bins and bones from domesticated animals. They determined it to be a community close to 10,000 people with no apparent hierarchy as all their homes were similar in size; small and made of mud and decorated with animal skulls. The archeologists had found statues of fertility goddesses in each grain bin, depicting an apparent reverence for the Goddess. This is what I want to create at Hawk Circle, but instead, as the voice of the feminine, I feel muzzled as hierarchy pursues. I don't know whether to feel grief or rage.

I sit down on a stone step, looking out over the ruins. Amazingly well-preserved mud huts are scattered throughout the site arranged in a similar fashion to a maze. I imagine the people, once a nomadic tribe, deciding to grow food, particularly wheat, and as a result, needing to create homes and communities to tend to the farming. It's an A-ha moment for me as I begin to understand the spiritual significance of bread. It represents food far beyond just nutrition. It's food for the soul as it was instrumental in bringing people together to create communities, and into an intimate relationship with the cycle of death and rebirth, the growing and the harvesting, sharing, working together, and tending to the crops that fed them. This was the very beginning of civilization.

My thoughts return to Hawk Circle and the joyful preparation of food in the farmhouse kitchen. It's a fairly small room, but nevertheless, people gather around the counter and enter into deep conversations while chopping vegetables and preparing meals. One summer, I made an outdoor cob oven with a few other women. It was an experience that I easily imagine women having here in Catalyhouk thousands of years ago. We created cob by dancing barefoot in a pile of mud, sand and straw that we used to sculpt into a big-bellied woman. I taught the women how to make bread, heat the oven with a small fire, and then bake the bread inside her belly. I think women are drawn to these experiences because it stirs our memories of the old goddess cultures. I treasure these moments, however small, because they are the moments when women gather and all other concerns drop away.

We stop at the Catalhoyuk visitor's center before getting back on our bus. The center displays images of many artifacts that are found at the site, all very primitive, nothing like the well-made pottery with intricate designs and colorful pigments that I saw in

Greece. Some look like stone or bone tools, but the most significant artifacts to me are the small statues of the mother goddess
that are found in the grain bins and inside the mud huts. She is
round-bodied with full, sagging breasts, a large, drooping belly,
and sturdy thighs with dimples at the knees. She sits in a chair with
feline heads as arm rests, which may be a throne, but most likely
a birthing chair, the epitome of fertility. I can't help but to feel that
my body is beginning to look like hers. I find her captivating, so
full of life and juiciness, but admittedly, I don't want to look like
her.

Back on the bus, we head to a small museum out in the countryside, near an ancient site. Its entrance is guarded by large stone
lions that stand at least 15 feet high. Before entering, Helena leads
us around to the side of the museum where they have well-preserved, stone carvings depicting sky beings.

"These are referred to as "stepping down" instruments. The sky
beings used them to lower their frequency so they would material-
ize on the earthly plane," says Helena pointing to small instruments
the figures are holding in their hands.

Oddly, this makes complete sense to me. My understanding is
that there was a spiritually advanced race of people who weren't
as deeply incarnated as primitive man, and the "stepping down"
instruments helped them to interact with one another. From what
I had read, many of them admired the more incarnated aspects
of the primitive man. While they, themselves, were spiritually advanced, primitive man made beautiful and useful tools. And they
also experienced life with deep emotions — something the sky
beings lacked.

I feel dizzy walking through the front doors of the museum. I
head to the back, separating myself from the group where more
lion statues and ancient artifacts line the hallway. The dizziness
subsides, but is replaced with a feeling like someone has removed

a helmet from my head that I didn't even realize I was wearing. I reach for the necklace that hangs around my neck, rubbing its stone pendant. Our group member, Deborah, works with crystals and stones and had given me the necklace just before our visit to the museum. I feel it's contributing to my experience.

Every belief I have is removed—the pure mental realm void of all human construct. I walk slowly around the museum, careful not to make any sudden gestures for fear I'll be jarred from my current state and the doors to the portal will surely slam shut.

I experience a sense of vast space, void of all attachments and beliefs of the human mind. I especially notice being free from my strong beliefs around being a good mother. *Am I walking in the land of the sky beings with no concrete form?* I realize that there's so much to our universe that my human mind can't possibly comprehend. My constructs, my beliefs, are all just a safety net. A container of sorts that helps me feel safe, brings order to chaos, and helps create my individual identity, but no more than that.

The more I realize I know nothing, the more I feel closer to the truth.

This experience is so different than my usual heart-opening experiences that reduce me to a puddle of tears. I have no emotion, other than wonder and amazement.

An incredible feeling of freedom washes through me. I imagine what it would be like to create my life from this mindset — no limitations whatsoever to serve as obstacles or hurdles along the path. I'm like a kite seized by a gust of wind, free of attachments and form. At the same time, I also imagine leaving a trail of destruction in my path, because, while my beliefs create limitations and separation, they also hold me to a moral and ethical code that creates order and a sense of belonging to a tribe of other like-minded people. I have an appreciation for both the freeing mindset of the star beings and the devotional caring mindset of humans.

Wow, I never realized how I've put so much stock in what I believe, but it's all something I've conjured up to feel safe. There's no greater truth to our beliefs, no one way that is right or wrong.

As we board the bus, I grab a seat next to Helena.

"What juicy news do you have for me today, dear Treeeesta?" she says as she puts her arm around me, pulling me close.

I chuckle, noticing that our snuggles on our sacred journeys together are synonymous to sharing a profound experience or big A-ha! moment with her.

"I have to tell you what I experienced while inside the museum," I say.

"I'm all ears, sweetie," responds Helena as she leans closer to listen to hear my story. "Ahhh, yes. What do you feel this experience taught you?" she asks.

I pause, wanting to choose my words carefully.

"It taught me the reality of beliefs and the freedom I have to choose what I want to believe in. I think I'll be more inclined to take a close look at my beliefs as to whether they support my growth or limit me. And when the latter, let go of them much easier." Helena nods her head in confirmation.

"There was such a oneness in the realm I walked into," I say.

"Say more," says Helena.

"Well, because it lacked the concrete form of beliefs, it felt void of the strife and internal conflicts. There was no polarity of right and wrong, good or bad." Again, Helena nods.

"Yes, that's it Treeesta. Our internal conflicts are our beliefs that get in the way of who we really are and the original state of oneness," says Helena.

I shift to a seat at the back of the bus and for the remainder of our bus ride, I contemplate the beliefs that are passed down by my family.

Do they support who I want to be or get in the way of who I want to be?

Do my beliefs create union or separation?

Driving out to visit the Sumela monastery high in the Pontus mountains, I think about my path as an initiate. I've traveled deep into my roots, bringing consciousness to the parts of myself that remained hidden and buried underground. I'm comfortable with this work, no matter how hard it is at times. It feels familiar to me — a process of remembering more of who I am.

"Is it okay if I sit with you? You look deep in thought," asks Gretchen. Gretchen is one of our younger group members, a newly certified chiropractor from Boston. This trip is a graduation present to herself.

"No, not at all. Have a seat," I say, picking up my bag and putting it between my legs.

"I want to ask you more about what you meant when you were talking about the sacred marriage last night at dinner," she says.

The night before, I had shared the story of my meeting Ricardo and the dream I had of us on a boat and receiving the message about the sacred marriage.

"It's about bringing union to all the different aspects of yourself that have remained separate," I say, carefully choosing my words. "It's not necessarily a path of romance like most think," I say, chuckling.

"Why's that?" she asks, with furrowed brow.

"Well, because typically, the parts of ourselves that we need to reclaim are mirrored back to us by our partner. And they can be difficult reflections that take time to work through," I respond. "Relationships are great for shadow work," I add.

"What's shadow work?" Gretchen asks.

I grab a pen and sketch out a tree on the back of a napkin.

"See the roots? When you do this kind of work, heal your shadow or unconscious parts of yourself, you are growing your roots. And like with actual trees, a strong root base grows a tall tree with strong branches," I say, hoping it makes sense to her.

"Yeah, yeah, I get that!" Gretchen exclaims excitedly.

"The New Age movement has uprooted us with its continual striving for the light. We need to explore the darkness, otherwise, like a tree, we topple over. It's just not sustainable." I say this with such strong conviction as I'm reminded of so many New Agers I've encountered that drive me crazy with their false sense of positivity.

Our conversation comes to an abrupt end as our bus pulls into a small parking lot at the base of the Pontus Mountains. Stuffing an apple into my pocket and grabbing my sweater, Gretchen and I leave the bus to follow the path that leads pilgrims up the mountain to the monastery. It's a majestic foot path, surrounded by a dense forest of evergreens that cling to the sides of the steep cliffs. The mountains are massive, located in the northern side of the Anatolian peninsula, near the Black sea where ancient Greeks fished and grew hazelnut trees and a variety of fruits.

The stone monastery, once part of the ancient country of Pontus, is perched on a cliffside and is undergoing reconstruction. Tired and breathless, I reach the entryway and am given a hard hat in case any crumbling pieces of stone fall. Inside, there are paintings on the walls still imbued with bright colors dedicated to the Virgin Mary. As the legend tells, an icon of the Virgin, that was once in Athens, Greece, and is said to have been created by one of Jesus' disciples, mysteriously made its way to a hollow in the Pontus Mountains. The icon was initially found by two hermits and is believed to have miraculous powers.

Clearing some small rubble out of a corner in the furthest back room, I sit down on the cold, dusty stone floor to meditate, facing the icon of the Virgin Mary, painted black, which isn't how she is usually depicted. I wonder if she actually had originated in Egypt and came from the worshipers of Isis. I imagine what it was like to construct such an incredible place, delicately perched on the side of a mountain.

As my thoughts transport me to another time, I imagine the residents of the ancient monastery living a life of simplicity, entering into daily prayer and ritual high in the mountains and veiled by clouds.

Suddenly, everything grows quiet and still. Chatter from other members of our group and the distant sound of the men working all fall away. Time stands still.

The Virgin Mary appears out of the mist, her form transparent.

"Hello Mother," I say, my voice quivering.

"Come out of hiding child. Show the world your light," she says, her voice deep with an accent I can't place.

Tears pool in my eyes as I realize I've been hiding all my life as though watching life from behind a thin curtain, interacting in a way everyone expected. I pray for guidance, for an opening to reveal more of who I am. My sacred self stands quietly hidden, concealed in a carapace, safely tucked away from the world. The Virgin Mary extends her hand into my inner most sanctuary, gracing my heart with her presence and inviting me to shine. The faded background of conversations from our group members and the nearby workers returns, pulling me back to the here and now as the Virgin Mary fades back into her wooden form.

I remain seated. Stunned, I look over my shoulder and wonder if anyone else saw this. But no, the rest of the group members are quietly talking amongst themselves as they study the beautiful paintings on the old, cracked walls.

I don't fully understand her message of coming out of hiding, but I can feel the truth of her words. I sit for a while longer contemplating my life and wondering what new paths are going to present themselves to me when I return home. My thoughts wander to our land and to Hawk Circle. I want more of a monastic feel at our place, a slower pace and more time for contemplation. In front of me stands the statue of the Virgin Mary and to my right, a few yards away are men hard at work restoring the old monastery. I realize that I need to stop butting heads with the men at Hawk Circle and recognize the hard work they're doing. Like the Turkish men here, they are restoring our place, and it's okay they don't share in the same vision.

Our visit to the Pontus Mountains brings us to the end of our sacred journey. My visit to Turkey has been an immersion into a vibrant, earthy culture, with aromatic smells of spices from the markets, and hand-woven carpets, intertwined with rich, vivid colors. I loved the prayers chanted from the mosques each morning. It's magical to imagine everyone waking to the same prayer being sung over the land. It reminds me of our place when we have a group visiting. Someone plays a flute or drums as the sun rises to wake up our guests.

As my plane lifts off from the Istanbul airport, I think of the in-between place—between heaven and earth. The duality of earth and sky, dragon and dove, man and woman. I see why Helena referred to this trip as "The sacred union." It's a place where the roots of civilization began in union with the timeless sky beings.

Chapter 16
Return to Avalon

Like the center of a rose, I am held deep within the folds of soft petals, hiding in the safety of my own flesh. As the warm rays of the sun begin to work its magic on me, the folds of petals begin to awaken to the sun's gentle touch, opening, softening, revealing more of who I am.

I stand back to take in the beauty after lighting the last candle on the table. An intricately woven tablecloth of deep red and turquoise that I brought home from Turkey is spread out on our table with simple white plates, burgundy candle sticks and little white lights strung overhead. An enchanting space for our meal. It's a chilly night on the brink of winter and our wood stove emits a soft glow. Our instructors who are living in the farmhouse are coming over for dinner.

They're such an awesome group of young men, on their own sacred journey staying at our place, way out in the wilderness with little contact to the outside world. It's like an extended vision quest for them, an experience that not many young men would choose. To me, they are the Arthurian knights seeking the grail, searching for answers to life's big questions. They have a real goodness to them. I can see it in their eyes, a brilliant light revealing old souls, true guardians of the grail, old time warriors and protectors of this world. I create a meal for them with this in mind, honoring who

I see them to be. As I knead the soft, warm dough for bread and sprinkle freshly chopped herbs over the venison roast, I imagine hosting the Knights of the Round Table. Soft music playing in the background, hot cider on the stove and a warm apple pie on the counter fills our home with a sense of magic. I light a small candle and place it in a rawhide lantern that Ricardo has made and hung outside by our front door.

Our instructors inhale the sweet and savory aromas as they walk into our kitchen. Their usual quick pace slows as they see the candles, and they enter our home with reverence and curiosity. At the table with the rest of our family, they remark on the deliciousness of everything they taste, savoring not just the food, but my love and devotion that I've poured and churned into it that feeds their souls. Most of the dinners they cook for themselves involve ramen noodles with little else.

With full bellies, we sit around the dinner table talking and laughing and sharing stories. They ask me about my trips. I stumble on my words. It's only been two months since I returned home from Turkey, and I never know how much to share about my intimate experiences. They're hard to explain, and I struggle to find the words. *Are they just being polite, wanting the short answer, or do they really want to know details?* After sharing a bit, they press for more and it becomes apparent by their quick glances with one another that they've been talking amongst themselves trying to figure out what actually goes on when I venture off on one of my sacred journeys.

They listen intently as I share more stories and describe the power points on the earth that facilitate healing and places where the veil between worlds is thin, and where you can access other dimensions. They listen with curiosity, asking questions. I tell them that I also see our land as a sacred site and that it holds a power that accelerates consciousness very similarly to some of the sites I visit.

Our instructor, David, seems particularly curious. But I can't tell if he's sincere or is looking to challenge me. He has sort of a "bah humbug" attitude. I'm used to bumping up against people's rational minds that want to discount every idea or experience that's out of their normal, everyday existence.

By the end of the evening, to my surprise, they ask me if I'd be willing to meet with them once a week and teach them. Having worked with so many of the young women that came to Hawk Circle, I welcome the opportunity to work with the men. I imagine the Knights of the Round Table and King Arthur himself, humbly asking a priestess of Avalon to teach them, huddled around a fire on a cold winter's night sipping an herbal tonic she's made.

It's proving to be a long, cold winter, but every week I traipse through the snow, down to the farmhouse and spend an evening teaching our small group of instructors. I teach them mostly about the sacred marriage and bringing union to our dualistic natures, and how to recognize and work with their own shadows and wounded parts of themselves. They ask great questions, and my time spent with them feels really sweet. I meet with them throughout the winter right up until the snow begins to melt.

The goldfinches are back at our feeder on our deck, a sure sign that spring has officially arrived. Our pond is overflowing and, from inside the house, I can hear the rushing of the cold spring water coming down off the mountain. The air feels so fresh and alive with the smell of the softening earth and tender green garlic mustard sprouting in the field with clumps of bright yellow daffodils scattered throughout our yard.

Early one morning, I roll out of bed, grab my old hand-knit sweater, pull on my rubber boots, and head outdoors with Bradford just as the sun is peaking over the mountain. I love the early mornings here at Hawk Circle. Our land stays hidden in the mist, like a blanket of clouds lulling everyone back to sleep. It's quiet, and we venture down the road moving through the swirling mist as it dances around us, following us wherever we go. While Bradford is too old to dance with the mist, he walks next to me sniffing the scents the mist carries to him. The light of the morning sun streams through the fog shining on the tiny droplets of water turning the mist into a curtain of sparkling, diamonds. Spiderwebs spread out amongst last year's stalks of goldenrod look like dream catchers woven with silver thread. It reminds me of photos I've seen of the magical isle of Avalon, an island veiled by the mists of the sea and the heart of the Arthurian legends.

Bradford and I are just coming out of the white pine grove when we see David walking towards us.

"You're up early," I say.

"Yeah, I had a hard time sleeping. I saw you walk past the farmhouse so I thought I'd come find you."

His voice quivers, and he looks a bit shaken. Ricardo has trained our instructors well in tracking, so it was easy for him to see which way we went, following our tracks down the dirt road and off onto the worn footpath through the field.

He looks at me, holding my gaze for longer than I'm comfortable, and I turn away. He seems to want to say something and with anyone else I would have pressed on, wanting to know what it is that was troubling him. But for some reason, I don't want to know, so I continue walking and making meaningless conversation. When we get up to the farmhouse, I turn to continue down the road to our home, but reaching for my shoulder, David stops me.

"Hey, I've been thinking about that burial ceremony you did with Indigo. Would you do one for me?" he asks.

"Oh, yeah, no, I'd be happy to," I quickly answer as a voice inside my head yells the opposite.

Noooooooo! You don't want to do this with him. Why did you just say yes?

"When are you thinking of doing it?" I ask.

"Well, how's next week work for you?" he asks, his voice still quivering.

"That works. Early in the morning is best for me, before the kids wake up," I say.

We set a day and time for the ceremony, and Bradford and I continue down the road back home. I have mixed feelings doing a burial ceremony with David, and I'm not really sure why. I want to help him and support whatever is going on for him, but I have an unsettled feeling when I'm alone with him that I can't deny.

The week speeds by. I gather up blankets and an herbal blend for blessing David's burial ceremony. We agree to meet in the apple orchard below our house just as the sun is coming over the hill. It's a quiet morning and there's a warm breeze gently blowing through the trees. I feel nervous, but I often do just before entering into a sacred space or ceremony where the veil between worlds becomes transparently thin.

David is standing quietly in the grove of old apple trees, patiently waiting for me. When I approach him, I can tell he's nervous. He's softened since I started meeting with him and the other instructors throughout the winter. I begin to realize that his questioning wasn't about proving me wrong, it was his own desire to understand more, to open up to other ideas that his rational mind was constantly trying to dispel. It was his own questioning of himself that he was really at battle with. There are times where I realize how similar our spirits are as I listen to the ways he processes his feelings. He often has the same response to things that I remember having when I first started learning. But for some reason, I continue to have a lingering feeling of wanting to run whenever I'm alone with him.

He's dug a deep grave between two old, apple trees. I say a few prayers and sprinkle healing herbs into his grave, or perhaps better described as Mother Earth's womb. He slowly and very deliberately lays down. I carefully lay a piece of thin silk fabric over his nose and mouth, and with shovel in hand, take scoops of dirt from the fresh pile of soil and sprinkle it over him. I cover him until he can no longer lift his arms or his legs with the weight of the soil and only his nose and mouth are visible. I sit next to him praying for guidance and for his healing. It's interesting for me to be on the other side of this experience. I hold a space for both death and birth at the same time. Death of what no longer serves David, pain that he wants to let go of, and the renewal of his spirit that's waiting to be birthed. I sit for about an hour as he goes through his process. I want to do right by him, but all I can do is sit and hold the space and be his witness.

An hour passes, and David is ready to come out. On hands and knees, I begin scraping away the soil, freeing him enough so he can lift his arms and legs. He emerges as soon as his arms are free enough to push against the weight of the soil. I imagine it's what a bird must feel when it finally breaks through the eggshell, seeing the light of day for the first time. I wrap a blanket around him, remembering how cold I had felt when I came out of a burial. Both of us stand in silence looking at one another, feeling the tenderness of the moment. I'm in such awe of his process and his willingness to be so vulnerable and open.

"Can I give you a hug?" I ask.

Without answering me, he drops the blanket and opens his arms and pulls me close with apparent pent up passion. Our bodies fade into the landscape, and I see our luminous bodies of our souls become one. It's a deeply intimate moment that feels like an eternity, but really, only a few seconds. I feel completely naked and vulnerable. My soul bared to both him and myself. Suddenly I understand my previous discomfort with him. It was my own fear of this moment, feeling so exposed. We know each other from another time and place. That is apparent. Perhaps we were tantric lovers in a past life and our souls remember the safety of being in one another's arms.

"I don't know who you are to me. Are you my teacher, my mother or my lover?" he says with his voice shaking.

I freeze, not knowing what to make of his words or how to respond. My mind goes to the images of the Triple Goddess in Ireland, the maiden, mother and crone. He's seeing me as the Goddess. I've unveiled myself to him. It's the combination of the two of us, our souls recognizing one another and the power of our connection that opens my heart. I've never had an experience like this before, and it's difficult to take in. As we stand in awe of the moment, a gentle breeze blows in showering us with delicate pink blossoms from the grove of old apple trees. We both start laughing as the trees shower us with nature's confetti.

He tells me that for the past several months, he's been having dreams about me. Sometimes I'm like a mother, holding him, other times I'm teaching him about the mysteries, while other times we're making love. I can see his fear and his confusion in his searching eyes, wanting answers that I can't give. We part that morning, me returning home and him returning back to the farmhouse.

We had entered the mythical land of Avalon, or the region of *"Tír na mBan"* as the Irish call it. A land rich in apple trees where the goddess of the land imbues her visitors with her bountiful gifts. This was believed by some, to be the land where Maeve, the Celtic version of Mary Magdalene, was born. So much symbolism in this moment with our land and the roots of the Avalon mysteries.

My unfolding relationship with David isn't about the two of us being together, and we both know that. This we never question. It's about what the combination of the two of us can facilitate for one another, a deep healing of great magnitude. Sometimes at our community dinners I see him looking at me with such love in his eyes, and I quickly turn away. My soul feels naked like he can see past everything about me, all the layers of protection, my ego, and my persona. He sees my goddess self, and it's a gift to have someone see me on such a deep level. I need his witnessing to help pull me out of my cave of hiding. My thoughts go back to my trip to Turkey remembering the message from the Virgin Mary in the Pontus Mountains, "Come out of hiding," she said. I'm also a little disheartened. This is the experience I've been wanting, but assuming it would be with Ricardo.

As beautiful as this experience is with David, I feel like I'm rising and falling all at once. The more I open up to my own beauty and power, the more I become aware of my attachments and fears. I hadn't realized how afraid I am of being abandoned. I'm like a rose blossoming to the rays of the sun while my fears are like a wild morning glory, growing just as quickly with its tendrils wrapping itself around the flower, trying to climb and compete for the sun. The only thing I can do is to observe what's coming up for me and breathe through it as a way to let it go. I guess this is what coming out of hiding feels like. I'm walking out of my cave and all my companions of fear are trying to hold on for dear life wanting to keep me in the safety of the dark cave.

This experience is really a moment of destiny that while powerful, is but a brief encounter with the Divine. I like to imagine that before we are born, we make sacred agreements with friends and soul mates to have our paths cross at important times in our lives.

A crossing of paths that reminds us of who we are, wakes us up and propels us forward.

I know David is leaving Hawk Circle before he even does. One day we're hanging out, talking, and all of a sudden, my stomach feels like something is torn from me, a loss. My eyes fill with tears, and I look at him.

"You're leaving," I say.

"No, I'm not. I'm not leaving," he says defiantly.

"It feels like you are," I respond.

"Well, I don't know what you mean, because I have no plans to leave," he says obviously frustrated with my comment.

A month later, things begin rapidly changing for him. An opportunity presents itself that's instrumental in helping him pursue his dreams.

"I guess I am leaving. How did you know?" he asks.

"I felt it," I say smiling between tears. I have mixed feelings.

While I feel sorrow needing to say goodbye to him, I'm also relieved. The strong feelings between us have been challenging, even though I'm clear inside myself that we're facilitating healing for one another and it has nothing to do with a romantic interest. It's natural to assume a sexual relationship will follow in this kind of situation, but that isn't the case. Even though the experience is sensual, I know it's not meant to disrupt my present life and commitments to another. But regardless, I often wake in the middle of the night, heart pounding, afraid that I'm doing something wrong, going against my commitment to Ricardo. So yes, his leaving brings relief.

In the end, it's a teary goodbye for all of us. He's been such a big part of Hawk Circle, and our family adores him. He's been like a big brother to Matthew, Jessi and Javi. He's going to be missed in so many ways.

Chapter 17

The Sacred Union

I walk down the tree-lined path, feeling the soft moss beneath my feet. I make my way to the altar of the heart where many paths converge. Standing there waiting for me is my beloved. At first, I am the beloved's bride, but as we become intertwined, it is the Divine Child that emerges from our heart that now beats as one.

"Have you heard anything from David?" Kelly asks.

I almost choke on my sandwich. I hadn't heard his name in a while.

"Sorry, didn't mean to alarm you," Kelly says chuckling.

"No, that's fine," I respond laughing. "I just hadn't thought of him for the past few months, and you just caught me off guard," I say, motioning to the waitress for more water.

"But no, I haven't heard anything from him. I'm sure he's doing fine, though," I respond, sounding ambivalent.

"He's never been one to email or call," I add.

Over the past year, I had thought of David often. I have confidence our paths will cross again when the time is right. It's more of a deep knowing than a wish or a hope. What I don't realize is that it's going to happen sooner than I realize.

Our last camp for the summer is just ending and I'm preparing to visit Helena for a couple of days. I finish throwing some clothes into my backpack when the phone rings.

"Kids? Can you get the phone?" I yell as I'm walking down the hall.

Nothing

"Ric? Are you in the house?"

Nothing

Okay, fine, I'll get it.

"Hello?" I say quickly.

"You sound out of breath."

My heart leaps into my throat as I swing around with my backpack hitting the lamp and knocking it to the floor.

Shit!

"Hi, it's David," he says.

"Hi! Yeah, sorry. I just knocked something over. How are you?" I respond, sounding breathless.

"I'm doing good. Hey, I'm in the northeast for a couple of weeks and was wondering if I could swing by Hawk Circle?" he asks.

"Yeah, of course. When were you thinking of coming?" I ask.

"Would tomorrow be okay?" he asks.

"Yeah, sure, I'm not going to be here though. I'm just heading out to visit Helena," I say.

"Oh really? I'm not too far from her place. I'm staying with some friends. When are you leaving?" he asks.

"Actually, I was just getting ready to leave when you called," I say chuckling.

"Why don't you meet me at Sherman's Crossing? It's right on your way, and we could at least go for a walk and catch-up. I can always come out to Hawk Circle later in the week to see Ricardo and the rest of the family," he suggests.

"Okay, yeah, sure. I'll probably be there around 1:00, but I can't stay too long. I told Helena I'd be there in time to help with dinner," I say.

David and I are meeting just off the road on the way to Helena's on a hiking trail that's behind the house where he's staying. It's super convenient. I know exactly where he's talking about. It isn't too far from where I used to live, and the trail was one I hiked many times with the kids. I set my thoughts aside and go to find Ricardo and the kids. They're all down at the farmhouse hanging out with the staff. Javi's sitting on his babysitter's lap, laughing at one of our staff's silly antics. I smile. We're so lucky to have such a wonderful community of young people for the kids to hang out with. Especially Javi. Sending him to school never felt right but having him immersed in our Hawk Circle community feels right in every way.

"I'll be home tomorrow afternoon," I say, giving them each a hug goodbye.

Thoughts of David return as I settle into my drive. My heart pounds in my chest like a fast beating drum, competing with the rhythmic beat of Loreena McKennitt's Celtic song, *Night Ride Across the Caucasus*. Like the Caucasus Mountains that divide the Black Sea from the Caspian Sea, I'm on my own ride over the mountains that separate my life as wife and mother from my own Divinity. I cling to the experience that David and I had last spring, an unveiling and moment of truth that was a triumphant passage, like receiving a scholarship after years of hard work. It was a small moment in time that to a mystic, enduring the path is sweet nectar that nourished my parched soul and inspired me to keep climbing the seeker's mountain. Is David just another seeker on the path that my soul recognizes? Or is it deeper than that? Is he an ancient priest to the temple of the Goddess? A protector of the Grail? Whatever he is, our heart connection is undeniable — like the alchemical blending of two elements that transform into gold.

I stick my head out my window letting the cool wind blow away my fears. I'm approaching a threshold moment, the crossing over from one life to another only to return forever changed. I don't know what my meeting with David holds, but my uneasiness tells me it's something life-changing. I keep telling myself it's no big deal and that we're just going for a short hike and then I'll be on my way. But my heart is telling me something different.

Driving over the mountain pass, I slow down, looking for the pull off to the hiking trail where we plan on meeting. There's a split second moment where I consider driving right past and fight the urge to accelerate.

The words on the sign *Sherman Crossing* come into view and just beyond the sign is David. He's casually leaning against his car, arms folded across his chest. Seeing him feels like home. I hadn't realized how much I missed him. Once one tear escapes, the others quickly follow, and I reach for my sweatshirt to dry my eyes while turning the other way so he won't see. I park the car off to the side. Taking a deep breath, I step out of my car and into his arms as he's standing right there waiting to give me a big hug.

"It's good to see you," he says, looking down at me, his eyes a sea of blue.

"Yeah, you, too. You look good. Life seems to be treating you well," I respond awkwardly.

"Yeah, it's been good. I have lots I want to tell you about," he says.

We start down the hiking trail, a gateway into the mysteries of the forest. It seems like it was just yesterday that I was walking this very same trail holding Matthew's little hand, with Jessi in a carrier on my back, turning over every rock and collecting sticks along the way. The trail leads us deep into the woods, shaded by graceful hemlock trees, their branches caressing my skin like a lover's gentle touch. I take off my sandals feeling the soft golden needles that blanket the trail like my own red carpet. I reach up, gently touching the branch of a young white pine tree and smelling its sticky sap on my fingertips. I prefer nature's perfume to any store bought concoction.

I'm hoping the more we walk, the more comfortable I'll feel, but that isn't the case. The smell of the decaying leaves on the forest floor gives me some comfort, but otherwise I feel completely vulnerable. I don't know who to be. I'm not the teacher, the mother of three, Ricardo's wife, the director at Hawk Circle or the healer. There's no assigned position that I can rely on for comfort and no title to hide behind. Once again, I stand in front of him feeling vulnerable and exposed.

I listen to him tell me about the work he's doing and the life he's creating for himself. I share how our summer camp season was, but other than that, I'm held captive by my fears and few words barely escape. I want to tell him how much I miss him and how incredibly grateful I am to have this time with him no matter how short, but the words never come. The trail is coming to an end as we round the bend, and so is our time together.

A rain cloud hangs low releasing a fine mist that cloaks the leaves and the branches of the trees waking up the earthy perfume of the forest. My heart longs for another deep connection, but as I see my car in the distance, all hope abandons me. As we round the bend in the trail, something shifts. The birds chirping and the distant sounds of the cars on the nearby highway become silent.

Why do I feel like a little girl being sent away from home right now?

I feel like I'm about seven years old walking down the trail with David. It makes no sense. A single tear slides down my already damp cheek, followed by another.

"Why do I feel like you're a little girl right now?" David asks curiously.

"I know. I don't know why," I say, trying to hold back tears.

His being able to see what I'm experiencing, makes it all the more real, and my initial feelings of being sent away from home become more pronounced. I feel like a child being sent away from her family and the safety of her home.

"I can't let you leave like this," David says as he puts his arm around me and pulls me close.

As the rain cloud opens its flood gates, so do I. Dropping to the wet ground, my body heaves with deep sobs as I clutch the dark soil and burrow my face into the old, fallen leaves that litter the forest. I see in my mind's eye, the image of the Magdalene as I release the anguish of having lost the intimate connection with my own divinity. I am the bride in exile, banished from my own heart and the forgotten realm of heaven on earth. The loss I feel claws at my heart, tearing it open, exposing my despair.

I am ripped apart by my suffering, but it's through my broken heart where the light enters. I am no longer the little girl, but instead the Magdalene, the virginal bride.

I'm empty, hollowed out like an old, dead tree, and then the light returns. Every cell of my body reverberates the beauty of the forest as my tears transform from grief to tears of joy. Looking up at the trees that tower above me like guardians to the Divine, I see waves of pulsating, emerald-green light, the life force of nature. I see the same shimmering light on my hands, and as I move my arm through the air, I see my own web of life so magically intertwined with nature's and how my movements influence hers and hers mine. Everything sparkles with a vibrant life force that is more alive than anything I've ever witnessed or felt.

I'm the chalice, the holy grail, opening to the divine feminine and becoming one with the earth, the wholeness of the sacred marriage as the light of the Excalibur, the sword of truth, penetrates my core. The love I feel for all life is beyond anything I've ever known. I reach for David and press my hand to his heart. He looks at me with eyes of compassion and reverence and exclaims how incredibly strong he feels. He carries the heart of a Grail Knight, a protector of the Divine Feminine.

In the cathedral of the forest, I become the bride in union with the Divine. There's nothing I want more in life than this. All other matters of importance drop away, my desire for any other possessions in life pale in comparison to my desire for union with the Divine.

David and I are without words in this moment, yet know we have to say goodbye. Our brief time, destined to spend together in the woods, comes to an end. I tear myself away from him and this mystical, life changing moment. With a mixture of rain and tears running down my face, I say goodbye. I get into my car, and as I turn the key, Loreena McKennit, in her beautiful Irish accent, belts out her song, "Dante's Prayer" as I drive away.

I arrive at Helena's a half hour later and stumble into her kitchen, wet from the rain, dirt-stained jeans, and swollen eyes. She takes one look at me, sets down her wooden spoon she's stirring the pot of soup with and wraps her arms around me guiding me to her sofa while handing me a box of tissues. I tell her everything that has happened as she gently wipes away my tears and pours a cup of hot tea for me. I feel so dismantled, not knowing where to go from here. I plummet back to my normal existence. The double-edged sword of truth, carrying the power of polarity sliced my life in two. One side, the light of the Divine and the other side shadowed by my own lack of self-worth. As beautiful and abundant as the experience was, it shines the light on every aspect of my life that isn't aligned with abundance. The realization that hits the hardest is knowing that abundance and the Divine, previously experienced in separation, has been right here all along, shrouded only by a thin veil. I lived almost half my life separated from true beauty. It's like a piercing light that makes its way to the deepest corners of my life, revealing such a potent contrast to my potential and my actualized self, the love of the divine and the grief of loss.

Helena and I abandon the idea of making anything more for dinner other than her soup that is already on the stove. We sit at her kitchen table tearing pieces of bread and dunking them into our hot bowls of curry squash soup while sipping red wine. We talk into the wee hours of the night. I climb into bed, tired and so grateful for everything in my life — my beautiful children, Hawk Circle and our land, Ricardo and his acceptance of my unusual pursuits, David and my deep friendship with Helena.

"There are many paths that lead to union, Treeesta. It is not for you to lose this magic, but to continue on the journey knowing a greater truth. Go home, return to your life and cultivate the abundance you know to be true. Walk as a keeper of the Grail Heart," says Helena as I hug her goodbye the next morning.

Chapter 18
Divine Child

I listen to your wisdom deep within me. I feel the purity of your heart. Guide me, divine child, in creating my life that is aligned with your truth, your love, your light.

The soft cooing sounds of the mourning doves outside my window gently wake me, and I roll out of bed, pull on a pair of leggings, a heavy, wool sweater, and my L.L.Bean boots and go outdoors. Over the past several weeks, I've woken up early, needing time to contemplate and sort through unexplained emotions while the rest of my family remains asleep. I give a quick whistle to Bradford, and we head down the road to the river, our "little Nile" that winds its way through pastures and wetlands like a long, graceful snake.

The morning mist lays heavy in the valley, concealing the colorful, fall landscape behind its thick, white curtain. Two months have passed since my "Grail" moment with David and I'm sinking deeper and deeper into a descent. My world is shrinking in comparison to the expansiveness of abundance, and like the valley, I feel shrouded in a thick blanket of fog.

Little did I know, the brief walk through the woods with David was going to lead me to the wilderness of my heart where the Divine feminine resides. Returning home from that experience is no different than when I returned home from a sacred journey. I see my life with new eyes and am acutely aware of the ways my life no longer matches what I feel inside. The experience shone a very bright light on the enormous contrast between my potential and my divine self, and the reality of my day to day existence. But it also showed me what is possible for humanity — a new way of life on earth where the veil that separates our world and nature dissolves. What a different experience it would be for human beings if we lived in this space. I imagine a land of peace, abundance, and contentment. *Is this the ultimate union?* It's challenging not to attribute my Grail experience to David, but I know he only served as a gate keeper and guardian as I stepped through a sacred doorway into the Garden of Eden. It was a powerful moment for me to experience my full potential, and then to return home, roll up my sleeves and begin making the changes in my life to house all of who I am becoming.

Sitting at the edge of the river, I notice how it narrows in certain spots and it feels like the stream of abundance that flowed through me, now narrowing to a small trickle. My heart is closing down to a fraction of what it was. In my Grail moment, I saw the Divine in nature — its scintillating, green beauty and vibrancy, rivers of flowing energy that moved through and around me. Now, nature appears dull, quiet, almost like it's put to sleep, but I know it isn't nature, it's me.

I'm falling into a mundane existence.

I think back to my first sacred journey to Peru and what it felt like to return home. Nothing seemed to fit anymore. All I wanted to do was change the world around me and make it more conducive to who I was becoming. At that time, it was the school my children attended that I wanted to change, but this time, it's much closer to the heart. It's easier to spend time imagining a different world, anything that is far from the self feels safe, but to look at my own life with a magnifying glass, peering into the areas where there are beliefs and patterns that are rooted in fear and separation is grueling.

My relationships no longer fit, particularly with Ricardo. I can't make love to him in the same way. Stolen moments that are often the only time busy parents have for intimacy leaves me feeling empty. If we don't have the time to cultivate a sacred heart connection, then I don't feel safe. To enter into lovemaking as anything less than Divine feels like a self-betrayal. It's the womb/heart connection. Ricardo and I hadn't really ever given ourselves time to cultivate a deep, emotional connection. We loved one another, but desire and passion were definitely at the forefront of our relationship when we first met. Now my passion feels hollow without having a more intimate, heart connection. Sometimes it feels like a curse more than a gift.

I experience greater disdain with the way Ricardo and the board are trying to grow Hawk Circle. I know their hearts are all in the right place, offering children wilderness experiences, but it reeks of the old patriarchal construct infused with fear and continually pushing forward, taking no time to contemplate or trust in the best way to proceed. I feel left out, along with the natural world. I want our growth at Hawk Circle to be a conscious collaboration with the spirit of our land, but I'm at a loss for words when it comes to explaining this to the board members, and I'm met with blank stares. I don't have the energy to fight it anymore. Along with the rest of nature at this time of year, I retreat into my inner cave to ponder what it means to live my life in alignment with my divine child.

I remember the story of when Merlin asked King Arthur whether he chooses the Excalibur sword or the Cup. Without hesitation, Arthur chooses the sword. He's grown accustomed to its power and can't imagine being without it. But Merlin knows, without the Cup, the sword becomes destructive, and the Cup without the sword becomes manipulative. This was the downfall of Camelot.

While Ricardo isn't wielding an actual sword, his words are sharp, and he denies my wisdom and insight. We grow further apart, and Hawk Circle suffers.

Helena had once talked about the statue of the Madonna with the child on her lap. She told me that while most people assume that it's Jesus sitting on her lap, the child actually represents a new consciousness, a new cosmology born out of the sacred union of the masculine and feminine. I feel like both child and mother, the child part of me afraid, needing the world to be more gentle, more kind, and the mother in me wondering how to change my life to make it more conducive to taking care of my divine child.

I hold a secret. A deeper truth of our natural world and for humanity, and I don't know how to share it or how to guide others into the experience. All I know is the pain of living in a world of separation grows more difficult to bear.

I don't know how to create the change I need both in my relationship with Ricardo and with our vision for Hawk Circle. It feels daunting, too heavy. I'm trying to penetrate an old consciousness and believe if I can create change in my own life at Hawk Circle, then I can create change in the world. I eventually surrender to the notion that lasting change takes time. Dismantling the old patriarchal system and aligning with balance initiated by the Divine Feminine is an evolutionary change involving other people, not just me, a 2000 year old paradigm of firmly rooted beliefs and patterns. I have no role models, no examples I can emulate. Everywhere I look, I find the construct of the patriarchal system and when I dig deep enough to understand reasoning and motives, I continually find the foundation of fear. It's disheartening. I'm impatient. I'm annoyed. And most of the time, I'm furious.

I feel disregarded, and shout, as Inanna once did to her king Dumuzi, "I AM YOUR EQUAL!" I want to shake Ricardo awake. I feel so betrayed. It's a deep wounding that leaves my heart to bleed.

I understand my part in the struggle. I focus my need for change onto others, mainly Ricardo. No wonder it feels like a daunting task, because ultimately, I can't force him or anyone else to change. When I dig deep into my own motives, I find the same underlying fear and I know this is where the change needs to begin. It needs to begin with me. More than once I scream for my sisters, and when that doesn't work, I journey into dreamtime in search of them. But to no avail, they are spread far and wide, and my search leaves me further disheartened.

I eventually realize that the only way to be effective in bringing about change is to BE the change and accept where others are at and have compassion. It does me no good to know the Divine. I'm essentially ineffective and frustrated all the time carrying the knowing of my experience and wanting to impress it upon others. In order for me to be effective, I need to carry both the sword and the cup in balanced union.

I only know the power of the out-of-balance masculine and I hate it. I feel bruised by it. My heart speaks of something different — collaboration with others and with spirit, allowing and flowing rather than forcing and pushing, being rather than doing, trusting rather than fearing, loving rather than hating, empowering others rather than having power over, surrendering rather than fighting. These are my heart's virtues, and I strive to embody my heart's knowing in every circumstance.

I set about dismantling the construct of fear in every situation. Matthew chose to homeschool instead of entering 6th grade at our local school. I intuitively feel he needs time to ponder and re-discover his love of learning. Trying to fill out the required homeschool reports to meet the school's expectations is tricky. On a few occasions I receive letters from the school saying that if I don't comply, they'll force Matthew to re-attend their school. Fear wells up inside of me, the kind you feel when someone in a position of authority has the power to alter your life against your wishes. I breathe through these moments, letting go of the fear that somehow I'm going to damage my son if I don't follow the school's rules and expectations, that he's going to end up ruined because of me. Sorting through my fears becomes a daily task, continually returning to a place of love and trust, refusing to make decisions from a place of fear. For the most part, Matthew is unaware. I protect him from any threatening letters from the school, knowing this would only instill fear in him as well. At times, fear takes over and I set rigid academic goals for him. He questions my reasoning, and the look in his eyes reveals him losing faith in me. I quickly recognize my actions as fear, take a deep breath, let go, and re-negotiate the academic agenda, coming from a place of love and trust in his own innate wisdom.

When Ricardo and I fight over the direction of Hawk Circle and ways to move forward, I step back and track my own fear. It is a continual discipline to align with love and trust. The area where I'm most challenged is with our financial situation. It mirrors to us the exact opposite of abundance. There's little flow, a feeling of great lack that's reinforced every month when I pay bills and continually end up short. The strangulation of financial struggle is exhausting, and my attempts to align with an abundant flow feels so futile. I continually examine my mindset, uncovering beliefs that are aligned with the mindset of not having enough. Enough time, enough money, enough strength, enough love, the mindset of being in survival. Ricardo teaches survival skills, so I compare this mindset to being in survival in the woods where the goal is to survive, not thrive, where your needs are just barely met.

It's an effort to turn my experience around. Rather than focusing on the money we don't have when I pay bills, I instead focus on gratitude for the money we do have. At first, my gratitude feels fake, but eventually, I genuinely feel grateful for whatever we have.

I also struggle to find my footing during Javi's emergency surgeries. As a result of having spina bifida, he's susceptible to having spinal fluid build-up around his brain and had a shunt placed in his head to alleviate the situation years ago. Man-made substitutes for body parts are never foolproof. There are times when the shunt fails, or he develops an infection, and we rush him to the hospital before seizures take over. The questions and insinuations by some of the doctors that my herbs or homeopathic remedies are somehow harming my son or are deemed ridiculous with no credence whatsoever is alarming. In his hospital room, I set up my own corner of natural medicines during his stays despite the looks from the doctors intended to condemn my own wisdom. All I want to do is support Javi's health the best I can.

I'm like a carpenter building a house design from a blueprint I've never seen before and whose architect is the Divine Feminine. It's challenging three of the biggest institutions we have in our country, our educational system, our healthcare system and the institution of religion.

The oldest and most ingrained pattern that blocks the flow of abundance is my pattern of caretaking. I come from a lineage of wise women, but we are caretakers through and through. A wonderful attribute except when taking care of others supersedes taking care of myself. This pattern is woven through all aspects of my life and as I discover, has many layers to it. It reveals itself in several ways, but at the root of it all, is a belief that I'm responsible for aspects of my loved ones' lives in areas where they need to take responsibility. I uncover this pattern in all of my relationships as a wife and a mother, and it's especially tricky since I'm in the role of taking care of my family.

Unraveling this pattern is a path all its own. With every revelation, I feel unburdened each time, freeing myself from an inappropriate tending to another person's needs, and instead, practicing loving kindness towards myself. It's such a significant aspect of my grail experience. Practicing loving kindness and compassion for myself is the filling of my own grail cup.

As I sit near the stream watching the graceful flow of the water move around and over the rocks, and the trees on the river's edge, gently dipping their frosty branches into the stream, it's so peaceful and so balanced. The water's ease as it flows reminds me of the feeling I had in my Grail moment. The water accepts the fixed positions of the rocks, and the stream carves a path that is far from being straight and linear. It shows no struggle, no resistance, and what really strikes me is its balance between flowing in and around and over, and at times forging its own path, a tributary where it carves its own way through the earth's surface.

Like the edges of jagged rocks that overtime are smoothed and rounded, influenced by the continual flow of water, the change goes unnoticed. It's so subtle, yet it's happening, like the change of seasons. The snow melts, the sun shines down and gradually the grasses return to a vibrant green, and one day we wake up and notice the leaves have unfolded and spring has arrived. Only the change I'm seeking isn't going to happen in a few weeks, or a season or even in a year's time. This change is going to take a long time.

What I'm seeking is evolutionary change and the most significant battle I face is with my own inertia. It's one thing to see what needs to be changed and even to intellectually understand how I want to go about creating change in my life, but it's another thing to do it. I stand at the gate of inertia where I often feel the weight of the world on my shoulders. I look at my family members, each so strong willed and stubborn in their own way, and I can't imagine how I'm going to carve out the world I want even within my own family. So many times I'm tempted to turn away, retreat to a world of fantasy, dreams and wishes, where everything feels lighter, but ultimately, I know hope and a wish won't get me to where I want to go.

Remembering Helena's words that I've heard her speak so many times, "This is the path of a grail leader, how to change what's inside of you to begin to change what's around you."

As Bradford and I head back home, I spend time walking in meditation with Mary Magdalene, asking for guidance and for the key to the Grail journey. The words that keep coming are *to soften, to allow, to accept.* I see myself moving through my life like the water in the stream, constantly flowing, not forcing my way through, not destroying everything in my path, but instead continual movement in and around and over, forging ahead, creating a new path.

I'm learning about love beyond my human fears and how to fill my own Grail Cup. And I'm learning how to lead through the power of my feminine nature.

Chapter 19
Grail Makers

*H*er patient arms wait for me. "Collapse into me," she whispers in my ear. She is the Divine Mother. Can I let go of all that I'm holding? I am a mother, but I am also a child, and I long to be held. My heart grows weary, and I have no choice but to surrender to her, falling, falling into her arms.

Driving home from dropping the kids off to spend the day with their grandparents and cousins, I slowly make my way down our long dirt road into Hawk Circle. The road appears to lead to nowhere but the forested mountain is where a sense of mystery and wonder draws you in. People come here, seeking out like-minded souls, safety, and a place where they can open and unfold to the birthing of new consciousness in our world, kind of like the stories I've read of Avalon. There's a recurring theme with Hawk Circle and the legendary island that re-surfaces every now and then. Like with Avalon, our place is invisible to many, despite our sign at the entrance to our road. People discover us when they reach a certain point in their lives and are compelled to seek out a deeper meaning to life, much like the knights seeking the Grail. And even then, the land remains veiled behind the mists, and the only way to reach the mystical island is by answering the ferryman's question correctly. While we have no ferryman guarding the entrance to Hawk Circle, we do have a bridge that carries visitors over our little

Nile river, leading to a knoll where a white pine tree serves as our guardian. It's here where the outer world falls away and visitors enter into our magical land. And like the mists of Avalon, our land is most often concealed by a dense layer of morning fog.

Over the years, we have a trickle of young apprentices that find their way here. Wise, old souls forging their own unique paths in the world. They're the young wizards, looking for training that involve wilderness and awareness skills, and herbal lore. Along with the small groups of children that come each summer from all over the country to attend our summer camps, Ricardo and I are surrounded by young people. Matthew and Jessi are getting older, and their friends spend a fair amount of time in our home.

Jessi often gravitates towards kids that come from challenging family environments. She loves having them over for dinner, knowing I'll give them special attention and offer them a different experience than what they are used to. I welcome them with a warm pot of tea with honey, a hot meal with lots of vegetables and candles softly glowing. They marinate in the tenderness and the care and the beauty that I offer. I give them an experience of nurturing for both body and soul that they can draw from for many years, and I hope at some point, they recreate for themselves. It's the same for our young apprentices. I observe them in our home, looking around with curious eyes, captivated by our home that provides such a distinct contrast to their own home environments. Ricardo's rawhide drums he's made hang from our wooden beams along with my drying herbs and our cupboards are filled with misshapen pottery bowls and mugs, the result of years of pottery classes both for myself and the kids. Goddess statues and amulets from my travels adorn our nooks and crannies, and a wooden tray of stone runes can be found in our bathroom. It's a place for people to come and get deeply nourished in a way that is authentic and earthy. Not like a fancy hotel or spa, but instead real, creative and imperfect; a place where the soul is awakened.

During this time, I spent a few days in Spain with Helena to visit La Moreneta. I was reading a book regarding France and there was a brief passage describing the Black Madonna statue in Montserat, Spain. The words tugged at my heart so strongly that I knew I needed to see her.

We arrived at the impressive monastery, Montserrat, perched high in phallic-shaped mountains. While the cathedral is an amazing work of art, it's in a nearby cave where I met La Moreneta. She was larger than life, reaching overtop the few people seated in the cave, while being anchored to the stone wall in the back. As she reached over me, her arms waving wildly around the people behind me, she bared her dark, brown breast in front of me. My child self drank in her elixir of divine milk, and I instantly felt grounded and in my body. A mother's breast and her milk help her infant to fully incarnate, pulling them into their bodies like the grounding energy of the earth. This is what La Moreneta gave to me. Nourishment for my Divine Child. I returned home renewed and replenished.

Since returning home months ago, I immerse myself in the energy of the mother. I've been a mother for many years now, but this is different. I begin to understand the power of the Divine Mother as a grail cup we can all drink from — nature, she is the ultimate grail. There's a theme emerging in my life, and it reminds me of a conversation Helena and I had while in Spain about the child on the Black Madonna's lap. The child symbolizes birthing new consciousness, and I'm continually "giving birth" to something new, and then needing to mother that part of myself so I can integrate the new consciousness into my life. With each initiation, my ability to hold a container for others expands.

As women, we are all Grail makers. The Grail, the mythic container where Divine love flows is many things. It's our heart and our ability to love. It's our womb, our physical container for creating and birthing life, and it's our homes where we physically hold the space to nurture and care for our families and others.

I feel more grounded and more aware of the consciousness of the Divine Mother and child. I'm able to see the wounded child in others, standing in the shadow of their lives, sometimes angry because of the lack of love and other times deeply lonely. My heart goes out to them with a compelling urge to embrace them all.

Ricardo, whose parents divorced when he was young, suffers in his own way. The wound of not having a positive male role model consistently in his life leaves him feeling inadequate to develop Hawk Circle to the level of success he desires. He carries tremendous stress every day because of this. I liken the situation to that of raising a child. My suggestions that we can't force Hawk Circle to become something that it may not be ready to be or force it to become something that *we* aren't ready for, fall on deaf ears.

Blending a family together has its own significant struggles. My ex-husband continues to be an imposing figure that lurks in the shadows. He doesn't have much to do with us because of physical distance. However, he's less than supportive, saying hurtful things to the kids and undermining my role as their mother, most of which I don't find out about until much later. The residual pain and grief, unmet expectations and sometimes misplaced anger from the divorce leads to a great deal of chaos in our home. I also see the effects of Jessi's birth where she was immediately taken from me, separated in an abrupt manner from the only safety she knew as a newborn. I'm surrounded by constant struggle that all stems from varying degrees of separation. Along with the responsibilities of caring for Javi and his special needs, it's overwhelming. I feel like I'm the only thread tying it all together, weaving my love for everyone through the pain, the grief and the open wounds. All I know is how to love each of them, but the one person I forget is myself. I don't always feel I'm doing a great job and sometimes, I feel the only thing I can offer is to infuse my home with beauty. I grow flowers and herbs, each year, digging a new garden bed until our home is surrounded by flowering roses, lavender, colorful lilies interspersed with several types of herbs. This is my remedy as my grail heart grows weary.

I turn to the womb mysteries, teachings from an ancient female lineage that ever since my first trip to France, over ten years ago, slowly permeates my consciousness. On that first pilgrimage, I explored the role of the sexual priestess and experienced the womb mysteries in the sexual realm. But now, this pertains to my power as a mother.

I begin to understand how a woman's womb holds and nourishes the unborn fetus as it grows while immersed in her energy field and bathed in her amniotic fluids. After the child is born, they no longer reside in our inner most sanctuary. Instead, they are contained by the energetic womb that extends well beyond our physical bodies and creates the physical container of our home. The womb mysteries, that I learned from the Black Madonna, help me recognize the power I have as a mother. Not just with my ability to love and nourish and influence my children on a daily basis, but to help transform our family and awaken their souls.

Just like our physical wombs, our homes are made up of all our beliefs and patterns. As I expand my consciousness, I expand the energetic container of my home. I see the struggles that my children or Ricardo face in different ways. I'm able to understand what their souls are trying to accomplish and feel I'm in a better position to support them. Every situation is a mirror that leads me to traversing my own inner landscape in search for the pattern that they're revealing. Sometimes I get caught in the snare of trying to teach them or intellectually support them through whatever they are going through much like talk therapy. The ineffectiveness of this method of support is evident, sometimes in backlash, but more often, the lack of change that follows. Again and again, I search inward for the answers and find that when I'm able to identify the pattern or dynamic inside myself, it shifts the dynamic for them with ease. It's a continual shift away from fear to an alignment with love and abundance. Even my relentless work with womb clearing and bringing harmony to my home has been tainted with fear. I realize that I'm driven to clear as much as I can, believing that this work will free my children from carrying on family patterns as they grow older.

But upon recognizing my underlying fear, I realize I need to soften and trust. Desperation is never a worthwhile energy. I ultimately know I can't push my own growth for the sake of my children, nor can I impose onto them what I think is important. I remember reading one of Aesop's Fables and the mother crab is teaching her young crab about pride and tells him that he should walk straight ahead rather than sideways. The young crab says to his mother, "Show me how and I will follow." This fable has always stuck with me. Telling our children how to be is never as effective as role modeling. All in all, there is nothing more nurturing for children than to be raised in a container of love. It's the elixir of life that anyone can drink from and be nourished. It's what we gravitate towards, like plants leaning in the direction of the sun.

Helena once said to me, "What we do for our children, we ultimately do for ourselves."

This work, as a mom and the womb mysteries of the Divine Mother, inevitably is helping me to cultivate the container and life that's conducive for my own divine child. It's an arduous path of loving all parts of myself and recognizing the divine in everything. Even when there's breakdown in our family, there is divine purpose, like our backyard compost pile. The decomposing and rotting food scraps are smelly and pretty disgusting, but it is an alchemical process that leads to rich soil that nourishes new growth. It's hard for me at times to allow the natural process of things breaking down, but because I trust this process in nature, I trust it in my home as well.

It isn't always easy to nurture myself through this process. It's much easier to pour my nurturing into my children, or their friends or our apprentices. I don't have a role model in my life growing up. I'm such an Earth Mama, and my mom wasn't. She was kind, loving, nurturing, and a compassionate person. When I was a child, she listened endlessly to my inner thoughts and process, and I appreciated her presence in my life. She was the epitome of the nurturing aspect of the Divine Mother, pure, gentle, loving, like the way that Mother Mary has often times been depicted.

But she wasn't aligned with her power, and in moments as a child when I needed the ferociousness of the Dark Mother standing up for me, protecting me, instead, I experienced her afraid to use her voice for fear she would upset someone or be seen as not nice. I was left having been betrayed by my own mother.

There are moments in my life with my own children where I'm the one who stood in a place of confusion, not clear as to how I should respond, fearful and uncertain, not wanting to offend or ruffle anyone's feathers. In these moments, I'm the one that left my child undefended as I wavered in my own power. These are the moments that haunt me as a mother.

I work hard at holding a healing space in my home and at Hawk Circle, and struggle to find ways to really nourish myself. Helena lives a few hours away and my visits are few and far between, but at her home, I can drink deeply. She's also an Earth Mamma, and I feel profoundly nourished there.

I also have a neighbor, Kat, who is an amazing hearth-keeper and Grail maker. Her home is built of straw bales, covered with white plaster and surrounded by herb gardens and fruit trees, much like the homes I remember seeing in Ireland. Walking into her home is like walking into the Earth Mother's sanctuary, filled with books, comfy couches and a long, wooden table where a warm pot of herbal tea, her own honey and a yummy soup filled with her garden vegetables await. Her kitchen cupboards are lined with Polish pottery and in the center of her kitchen where she prepares meals that warm the soul, is an old, wooden apothecary, oftentimes displaying an abundance of freshly harvested squash. During many quiet, winter nights, I drive down the road to visit her, always greeted with her warm smile and a mug of hot tea. We sit and knit and share stories deep into the wee hours of the night.

It's during this time that I recognize I'm not alone as a mother. That I'm part of the great cosmic mother energy, a matrix that I can rely on for support. Where before I often felt alone with the responsibility of tending to my family's needs on so many levels, now I experience a greater power where I can surrender over the pain or the struggle and know that my family is being held by not just me, but the Divine Mother. She is everywhere — in the meandering stream, the tall white pines, and the field of wildflowers. I call on her when my family struggles, ask her to hold them. I'm unburdened by her presence, and I, too, fall into her arms and bask in her love that renews every cell of my body.

Chapter 20
The Wings of Isis

A cross the oceans of time and from the far barren dessert, she calls to me again and again. Her call is a chilling whisper, coming from a time so ancient. Without knowing why, I turn away, resisting her until I feel her bird-like hand on my shoulder, long talons gently resting on my bare skin.

As our bus makes its way through the countryside, fields of sugar cane stretch as far as the eye can see parallel to the water's edge of the Nile. Old rickety wagons pulled by tired-looking donkeys line the road, heaped high with long, freshly picked canes. Small, clay brick homes are scattered alongside the road with a cow or sometimes a goat wandering in and out through the doorless entryways. Each small homestead has an outdoor clay oven for baking that are stained with black soot from their continual use. The earth-toned landscape is punctuated with stark white clothing and brightly colored rugs and blankets that hang on clothes lines to dry. I'm in awe of the organic way of the peasant's life here in Egypt, the only thing I find relatable, farmers growing food, raising animals and baking in cob ovens. All things I do back home.

A bare few months ago, I received a call from a friend I had traveled with several times. I was standing at my stove stirring a pot of oil and beeswax for a batch of herbal salve when the phone rang. She invited me to visit the land of the ancient ones with her.

Over the years, I resisted signing up for Helena's sacred journey to Egypt. I made all sorts of excuses as to why I couldn't go. I was never really sure why, but this time, with my friend's generous invitation to travel with a group she'd put together, and that Helena was leading, I had exhausted all of my excuses and agreed to go.

Most of Egypt feels very foreign, void of rolling green hills or lush forests that comforted me in the past when I traveled through places like Ireland or southern France, making home seem not that far away. Here, it's hot, dry and barren of lush greenery, with enormous temples that rise unexpectedly out of the sand dunes, as our bus travels through the desert. There's nothing familiar to grasp onto. There's no similarity to home, nothing recognizable. It's like being on another planet, leaving me to wonder if the temples were made by star beings or by other means than the hard work of humans. I feel ungrounded, my roots not knowing how or where to anchor.

The entryways to almost all the temples we visit are framed with giant pillars, adorned with multiple carvings and painted with a variety of colors that are vibrant and amazingly well-preserved. No walls are left blank; all are covered with hieroglyphs telling stories it could take a lifetime to decipher. I intuitively know the stories are more than historical details. They reveal initiatory rites that hold a consciousness as foreign as the landscape. I can't access them or feel them in the same way I have in other places. There are countless symbols that I also know are significant, but no matter how hard I focus, I can't gain any understanding. The carvings of faces, particularly the eyes, have almost an alien quality to them, each so detailed and very different than the stone carvings I've seen of spirals in the British Isles, or the Fleur de Lis in France. Even in Greece, which is so close to Egypt, there are spirals and water symbols and dolphins leaping, more feminine images than what I find here.

Arriving in Aswan and boarding a boat that carries us down the Nile eases my discomfort. The river's snake-like path reminds me of our own small river that runs in front of Hawk Circle, and I cling to its familiarity. The Nile gracefully carries our boat to temples that stand not far from its shores. Each temple similarly designed, depicts the path of initiation from the pilgrim's first step crossing the threshold into the mysteries to the very back of the temple's innermost sanctuary, open only to the adepts.

Our first visit is to Isis' temple for a sunrise ceremony. My alarm wakes me up at the crack of dawn, wrenching me out of a deep sleep. I hurriedly pull on my jeans and sweater and slip on my sandals. I meet our group in the lobby of our cruise ship before boarding a small boat that takes us to Philae, a tiny island, home to the Temple of Isis.

I wrap my scarf around my head and neck warding off the chilly morning air as our boat weaves in and out of the tall reeds through the gentle current of the Nile. Only the soft moon light reveals our passage, and I can barely make out the shapes of buildings in the distance. Coming around a bend, beyond the tall reeds, I see, silhouetted against the silvery-purple sky, just footsteps from the shore, the majestic presence of the temple.

We climb out of the boat and in a hushed silence, follow our guide Sarwat Hegazy and Helena along a small foot path and across the expansive temple square. The sun has yet to rise, and my eyes have a hard time adjusting, not quite trusting what I'm seeing as everything slips in and out of the shadows. We walk through the main entryway of the temple on our way to the innermost sanctuary. I pause, questioning my worthiness, feeling like a priestess who has left the temple and has been gone too long. *Am I going to be welcomed back?* I know *of* Isis, but I don't know her in the sense of having experienced her, other than her being considered both a priestess of the sexual mysteries and mother goddess. I have the distinct feeling I'm a returning priestess and need to ask permission before entering. I brace myself for the possibility that her answer will be a resounding "No!"

"I don't feel worthy of entering your temple, Mother," I say in a hushed tone, thinking back to when I journeyed into the dark realm of sexuality with Ricardo.

I slow my steps, waiting for her permission.

"Dear One, you do not understand. We sent you into the dark-ness because we knew you could and would bring light into the darkness. That was your mission. We honor YOU."

Sometimes messages are so big they're hard to digest in the moment. I don't feel worthy of her message and know it's going to take time to comprehend. I stand for a minute, not knowing how to respond or what to say, and then run to catch up with the group. One by one, we enter the inner most sanctuary in the very back of the temple, where Helena lights candles. The soft glow reveals hieroglyphs carved into the stone walls of the small, confining room. Images of the winged goddess appear to come to life as I listen to Helena's prayer, honoring Isis. At one point, I feel Isis standing next to me, an ancient, bird-like figure with large wings and talon-like hands that remind me of our chickens' feet. Chills run up and down my spine. I swear I feel her warm breath on the nape of my neck. I have the distinct feeling that Isis knows me far more than I know myself. It's unsettling, but I stay present with bated breath, and on edge, not knowing what's going to happen next.

We complete our ceremony just as the brilliant, orange sun rises over the Nile and the questionable shadows dissipate, revealing the inner beauty of the temple. I spend some time walking around, still sensing Isis' presence. But with the sun's light, she feels far less intimidating. As I wander about, revelations come to me. I think of her myth, a love story of loss, separation and renewal, and compare it to my own story. I've traveled around the world, gathering pieces of myself, as did Isis for Osiris, weaving the parts into wholeness, experiencing the pain of separation and the joy of resurrection. Vague memories flash in my mind of being in France with Helena. I remember, on a few occasions, hearing her refer to the Black Madonna as Isis. And I suddenly realize that it's been Isis all along that has called to me over the years. She is the dark mother from the core of the natural world. The manifestation of Sophia, the Divine Feminine. Her many aspects revealed in nature and the force that emanates through all of life. She remains veiled in obscurity and hidden from most, but in this moment, for me, Isis is unveiled. I now understand what the inscription on her temple means.

"I, Isis, am all that has been, that is or shall be; No mortal man hath ever me unveiled. The fruit which I have brought forth is the SUN."

Memories of my grail moment with David flood my mind. Our brief time spent in the woods when the world of nature revealed herself. That, too, was Isis! As I think back to my very first trip with Helena, to Peru, I see how She has been guiding me all along.

I feel lightheaded and dizzy as memories surface. Every journey ventured, every path walked, mountain climbed, cave crawled, was leading me here, to Isis.

I fall to my knees giving thanks to Isis, as my tears of gratitude spill onto the dry and sandy temple steps.

Later in the day, we visit Kom Ombo, a temple located in Aswan, Upper Egypt. It's dedicated to Sobek, the god of the Nile depicted with the head of a crocodile. The crocodile represents the dragon bloodline, which for the Egyptians, means the anointed ones or the messiahs. I think of the dragon lineage of the Arthurian legends and Arthur Pendragon, realizing there's a definite connection. As I walk through the gates of the temple, I hear someone behind me ask where the snake charmer is. The question grabs my attention, and I strain to hear their conversation. Usually a snake charmer sits just outside the temple gate. I've always been afraid of snakes as far back as I can remember. I welcome them in my dreams, as I understand their powerful medicine. But encountering them on the physical plane is a different story. I walk further into the temple, each step filled with trepidation and rising panic as my mind is engulfed with images of the snake charmer.

Helena checks in with me when she sees me starting to hyper-ventilate and directs me to a place off to the side to calm down. Images of a snake slithering up my body and wrapping itself around my neck, squeezing all the life out of me consumes me. I forced myself to confront my fear of snakes over and over again through the years. I sat outdoors with snakes that sunned themselves on the rocks just outside our front door. One time, a snake found its way into our bathroom when we first moved into our house. As it lay curled up in the middle of our bathroom floor, I sat with it and sang to it, determined to work through my fear. My drastic response at hearing the words "snake charmer" is confusing. I feel so defeated by my futile attempts to overcome my fear. My panic turns to anger.

Why am I being put to this test? What more do I have to do?

I'm afraid I have to reenact my worst fear and wrap a snake around my neck.

I sit on the sandy, stone floor of the temple, in a corner by myself.

"Just breathe," I keep telling myself.

As my fear and my fury subside, tears descend down my sunburnt face, and my breathing returns to normal. I hear the voice of the goddess gently speaking to me, or is it my greater self?

"Priestess, you are not allowing any room for your humanness. You do not have to face every fear as though your life depended on it. Honor your humanness and make your peace."

Honor my humanness?

Her words penetrate my thoughts, and I realize how hard I've been on myself over the years, feeling like I needed to be Super

Woman and conquer every fear. I've left no room for being human, always trying to do the work of the priestess in such a perfect way. I'm exhausted. I've been working so hard, going through one initiation after another and another and another striving for what? There is no end goal, ever.

I've faced every fear and every circumstance as an initiation, and I assumed this situation was no different. But I realize, there's a deeper layer of fear beneath my fear of snakes. The fear of not being perfect. I've worked so hard "training as a priestess," relentlessly self-emptying and cleaning out every dark corner of my psyche only to discover later this, too, is an illusion. An outdated mindset that holds me hostage, not truly enjoying what it is to be human.

This moment is about acceptance. It isn't about conquering my fear, it's about accepting my humanness. This takes me by surprise — a liberating moment. I'm tired of working so hard to bring change at home and at Hawk Circle. And my actions are really saying that I can't accept things as they are. This certainly isn't the message I want to convey, especially to my family. Desiring change and yet having acceptance for how things are in the moment is more aligned with love and less with fear. I let out a deep sigh. This feels so right and a much easier way to go through life. Acceptance doesn't mean giving up or letting go of the change I want. It just means that I accept everyone around me with love, including myself. That I don't have to push for change. I can create change with a sense of ease by accepting my imperfections and honoring my feelings.

A few days later, we arrive at our beautiful hotel in Luxor, The Winter Palace. It's a majestic hotel on the Nile that's built in the 1800's and once used as a winter retreat by the Egyptian royal family. With a somewhat faded grandeur, it speaks of an era long ago when dignitaries and kings visited. It's surrounded by gardens and stone walkways with an outdoor cob oven. An elderly woman, dressed in a white tunic with a brightly colored scarf tends its hearth, making homemade pita bread. From the hotel room I can see across the Nile to the desert, sand dunes cascading over the land with a few scattered palm trees near the water's edge.

I wake early the next morning, greeted by a warm breeze blowing off the Nile and the sweet smell of the flowers in the hotel's garden. I meet Helena downstairs for breakfast where we sit and enjoy a plate of falafel, hummus, baba ghanoush, and spicey, mashed Fava beans with eggs. We're to visit Karnak, one of the largest religious sites in the world and home to Sekhmet, the lion headed goddess.

"I think I'm going to stay behind and rest today," Helena informs me. "Will you lead the ceremony today at the temple?" she asks.

"Yes, of course. Is there anything else I can do for you?" I ask concerned.

"No, no, I'm fine. Just my stomach acting up," Helena responds in a quieter voice than usual.

I watch her as she leaves the table. Sarwat's eyes meet mine. He's been a long-time friend of Helena's and the only Egyptologist she'll work with. An unspoken knowing lingers between us. Helena's typical quick pace is now slower as she steadies herself with one hand reaching out for the backs of chairs as she makes her way through the restaurant. I haven't noticed her age catching up with her until now. It concerns me, but more than anything, I want to make sure I keep this in my awareness for the rest of the trip. I'm so used to being self-absorbed during the trips while entering deep into my own internal process, and I don't want Helena's needs to go unnoticed.

We arrive at the temple and follow Sarwat as he quickly guides us through the main part of the temple, across a stone walkway, to a small structure in the far back of the temple grounds. We come to a heavy, metal door which Sarwat unlocks that leads to a dark chamber.

After a brief ceremony honoring Sekhmet, one by one, each member of our group ventures into the dark alcove where Sekhmet stands, an awesome statue of the lion headed goddess. When my turn comes, I go in, shutting the heavy door behind me. Taking a moment for my eyes to adjust to the darkness, I kneel on the dirt floor before her. A small opening near the ceiling lets just enough light in to illuminate her, and I can see her gentle lioness face. Her eyes are filled with compassion, but her presence is one of pure power. Power that can either destroy you or heal you. I have no prior knowledge or experience with Sekhmet and don't know what to think. I am humbled, but afraid. As with my overall experience on this trip, there is no familiarity for me to cling to. There is no tangible quality assigned to her as is often the case with other goddesses.

As I sit in the dimly lit room, several feet away from her, my eyes meeting hers, I am acutely aware of any facade or veneer finish I have that hides my power. She urges me to embrace my power and not to shy away. She terrifies me, but I'm pretty sure it's my own power that's what really scares me.

Every now and then, the statue of Sekhmet appears to vibrate as if the energy she embodies is trying to escape and reach beyond the confines of her form. I'm convinced she's going to come alive, leap through the air, pounce on me, and tear me apart. I force myself to stay put, wanting to shift my experience, but nothing shifts. I dare myself before leaving her sanctuary, to reach out and touch her, almost giving her a hug, but not quite. As I slowly extend my arm, I gently lay my fingertips on her cool surface and can feel her subtle yet very evident electrical charge. I later discover she was originally a fierce warrior goddess that became a powerful healer, and I'm looking forward to returning home and working with her more intimately. I don't want to be afraid of my power, but there are times the warrior goddess rises in me, and the fear I see in other's eyes, makes me quickly shrink.

I particularly remember a time when a friend of Jessi's invited her to a nearby church camp for a week. When I arrived to pick her up on the final day, she ran into my arms, clinging to me for dear life. Apparently, Deacon Josephine, despite Jessi's teary-eyed pleas to call home, refused to allow her to contact me. The deacon had called me a few days ago saying that Jessi wanted to know how her brothers were since they had both been sick when she left for camp. She assured me that Jessi was doing fine and enjoying camp, but the opposite was true. I marched into her conference room where she was meeting with her colleagues. Fury rose up through me like an explosive fire, and I felt my 5'3" body grow ten feet tall. I unleashed the goddess' wrath. When I saw the fear in her eyes, I winced and reigned in my anger. I didn't want to scare her, but I did want her to know my disapproval for both lying to me and prohibiting my child from calling home. I find it challenging to carry both the heart of an empath and the heart of a warrior. But here's Sekhmet, being both.

One of our final visits is to the Temple of Dendera, where the goddess Hathor, wearing her headdress of cow horns, is revered. As is evident by "reading" the beautiful and colorful hieroglyphs, she is the goddess of passion and joy, another aspect of Isis. Her temple reveals a life centered around music, dance and agriculture. Images of feasts and festivals and all the animals that are raised as part of the community are clearly depicted throughout her temple. This is how I imagined Hawk Circle to be.

As I stand in awe, I feel the pure abundance that Hathor represents. Some believe Hathor is older than Isis and has stood in the shadows far too long. Others believe she is an aspect of Isis, as are all other goddesses. No one really knows, but I do feel the consciousness that Hathor represents is a return to the land for our sustenance and a return to community, celebration and joyful abundance. She is the joy experienced when we live having brought union to heaven and earth.

After our group returns to The Winter Palace, we pack our bags and head back to Cairo for our last two nights in Egypt.

On our last full day, we head out before dawn to the Great Pyramid, for our very own private visit to the King's Chamber. A palpable stillness hangs in the air as we approach the pyramid in the dark. The sun still asleep below the horizon's edge, but the air is already warm.

The majestic Great Pyramid stands proudly on a plateau above the desert. Like the other temples, it takes my breath away, so incredible, that I struggle to embrace the experience. So many extraordinary wonders will take me years to fully absorb them.

With Helena and Sarwat leading the way, we approach the pyramid that's silhouetted against the deep blue, morning sky. We climb stone steps that lead us through the wall of the temple. We enter through a small, obscure door that hardly seems fitting for one of the greatest wonders of the world. Inside, it's deathly quiet. No sound from the outside world can penetrate. With small lights, dangling from above, illuminating our way, we begin our climb up the narrow passage that leads to the King's Chamber. Several times I pause, convincing myself to keep climbing and not succumb to my feeling of claustrophobia. It's a narrow passage with areas requiring us to hunch way over as the ceiling above us is only a few feet high. When we finally enter the chamber, the awesomeness of being inside the pyramid is both overwhelming and exhilarating. Our small group quietly finds places to sit and meditate, receiving in the power of the pyramid.

Leaning up against the wall, I'm relieved by the coolness of the stone after making the arduous climb. I close my eyes, taking a few relaxing breaths and enter into the space between worlds. To my surprise, in my meditation, I see Ricardo walk in, carrying Javi with Matthew and Jessi following. My initial response is one of excitement feeling that we're all going through an initiation together. I watch them come over to where I'm sitting and settle in next to me, and I quickly calculate in my mind the time of day back home and realize they're all asleep in real time. My attention quickly returns to the entry point where I see my ex-husband furiously trying to get through the door. He's filled with rage. It takes me by complete surprise. There's no way I'm going to let him interrupt this moment. I call in the guardians of the temple to have him escorted away. Immediately, very tall warrior-like figures appear, pulling him back from the entryway, preventing his passing. I'm both relieved and curious. This isn't the experience I anticipated having inside the Great Pyramid.

I open my eyes and look around the King's Chamber. Everyone else is sitting still in meditation. I lean into my experience trying to understand it more. I feel Dan's anger like a cloud of chaotic energy with darting spears and recognize it as the energy I've been dealing with at home. It's sometimes difficult to get perspective on what is happening when I'm at home dealing with it day to day. With distance, I see how his anger has been infiltrating our home like an over flowing stream that I've been trying to manage and diffuse all the time.

This experience confirms what I've felt for many years. His anger towards me is far greater than divorce residue. This has more to do with my growing power and extends back to a lifetime long ago. I was curious as to how this experience on the non-physical realm is going to manifest on the physical plane.

I'm pulled from my deep thoughts when Helena comes over and taps me on the shoulder. She motions to me to climb into the sarcophagus that's positioned in the center of the chamber. It's a granite sarcophagus, about six feet long. How they ever got it all the way to the top of the pyramid, I'll never know. But then again, many questions and mysteries remain unanswered regarding the pyramids. Grabbing hold of the side, I climb up and into the sarcophagus. I lay down and close my eyes. While the King's Chamber is notoriously referred to as a burial chamber, I don't belief there's any truth in that. It feels more like an activation point for our light bodies and perhaps astral travel. Some claim the pyramid to be a massive generator, having been built with very specific stones to emit a tremendous amount of power.

Lying in the sarcophagus, the hard granite becomes like water giving me the sensation of floating, rocking back and forth on gentle waves. The point above me appears as a portal to the stars and I feel them calling to me. Perhaps this is one of the reasons Egypt feels so alien to me. I'm used to diving deep into the earth and working with the Mother Earth goddesses, but now, my attention turns towards the stars, another home, far from the earth. Floating in the energy of the sarcophagus, in my mind's eye, I see stars dance, changing from one constellation to another as if putting on a show. A particular star calls to me, shown brighter than the others, and I have the strange sense it's calling me home. My breathing stills as I connect with the one star, its light magnifying my own light. I'm brought back to my body as I feel Helena's warm hand on my forehead, letting me know it's time to leave. A bit wobbly, I climb out of the sarcophagus.

With deep gratitude for our experience, our group descends down the long flight of stairs out into the sunlit sky. The plateau now has many tourists just arriving, and we make our way to the Sphinx that rests just below the pyramids. Sitting between her giant paws, Helena begins telling us about a hidden library believed to be in the Sphinx.

"It is said that the library will be revealed only when humanity has reached a tipping point where the majority of the people care more for the good of the whole than only for themselves," she says with apparent enthusiasm.

"Do you think it will be revealed in our lifetime?" I ask.

"Yes, I do, most definitely," she responds confidently.

It's hard to believe at the time, since Bush had been re-elected for his second term and problems in Afghanistan ensue. The general consensus is that our government's involvement is purely self-serving. But I pray that what Helena is saying is true.

Later that night, after getting my suitcase all packed for an early morning flight, I walk to the lobby of the Mena House where we're staying. Through shiny beads that drape the large windows, I can see the Great Pyramid, illuminated by lights against the night sky. I have a sense of an inner library within me - knowledge of Egypt's greatest mysteries. Perhaps they are memories stored in my DNA. I trust in time, they'll be revealed, but for now, they remain an elusive mystery.

We leave for the airport early the next morning. As our bus heads out of old Cairo, I turn, one last time, to see the pyramid off in the distance. The sight is difficult to describe. Its massive presence radiates throughout the landscape like a god having landed from the stars, the epitome of otherworldly power, quietly sitting in the backdrop of a bustling city.

Chapter 21

Healing Separation

With golden thread, I weave together the tears of separation. Every stitch infused with love, dispelling fear, creating my life's tapestry of a new world where separation is but a distant memory.

The worst thing we've done is to put heaven in the clouds. And the very worst is believing hell is on earth. That one truly breaks my heart.

It's been a few years since I returned home from Egypt, and like most initiations, there is always a time of integration. Typically, the integration requires a year or two, but with Egypt, it's been an endless and gradual unveiling of consciousness that has gone on for several years. There are no sudden "a-ha" moments. Rather, it's like standing on a shrouded landscape that changes shape and texture so languorously, I'm not even aware of the change. Only looking back years later can I see the difference. Subtle changes in awareness that have the most profound impact.

Somehow, it felt easier before. When I started down this path many years ago, I was acutely aware of the task at hand during an initiation because it presented so much drama. Boundaries were crossed, lies were spoken — the pain and fear were so visceral that the path through the thicket was clear, still challenging and at times scary and painful, but clear. Now, I walk through the landscape of my innermost mind with no vivid signposts, no drama pushing me in one direction or another. There is no imagined "enemy" that I need to face, and no part of me that needs rescuing. Just a single thread to follow — the one aligned with love.

"What would love do or say in this moment?" I ask myself when faced with struggle.

This isn't about finding my voice or leaving a situation. It's quite the opposite. This is about learning how to change my perception of the landscape I currently stand on, to have a completely different experience. With Hawk Circle. With Ricardo. With my work in the world. It's a process of untangling my innermost threads that tie me to fear, to the old fabric of the patriarchy, and old stories that I've believed were true. It's a path of altering realities.

I am weaving a new world paradigm — letting go of the threads of fear and picking up the golden threads of love and weaving them into my thoughts, my beliefs, and my life. I feel like the Divine Mother with the child, sitting on my lap, a new cosmology.

It's the end of summer. The morning air is cool. I grab my sweater before heading out for my morning walk. With a quick whistle, my new pup, Libby, comes bounding out of the field of purple asters that cover the hillside, and races ahead making sure she's in the lead. It's been a few years since Bradford passed. He died a good death, on a bed I made for him in our kitchen. I held him in my arms as he took his last breath. Three years later, I yearned for another furry companion. She came to me in a dream one night, so clearly, standing in the dark, like a golden angel appearing out of the void. I spent a couple of weeks looking for her on breeder websites, but nothing felt right so I abandoned my search. Then one day, I had the sudden impulse to call a local vet. The woman who answered the phone had just heard from a breeder not too far away that had a litter of golden retrievers ready to find new homes. She gave me her number, I called, and arranged a visit. Javi and I drove over the hills to the next county to take a look. Little Libby was the only girl left in the litter and came home with us that day, full of piss and vinegar and testing every bit of my patience.

We wander up the trail behind our house. The landscape is ablaze with a bright yellow hue as a result of the goldenrod in full bloom, interrupted here and there by deep purple asters, fading chicory and pink spotted knapweed.

We head into the woods where there's a cluster of old apple and hawthorn trees. It's a place I feel more connected to the Dark Mother and Mary Magdalene. The ground is always damp, with no visible stream of water, but instead many underground springs. It has the same energy as some of the old wells I remember visiting in Ireland years ago. A palpable feminine presence flowing deep underground, into the crevices of the earth, slowly rising and saturating the forest floor, littered with decaying leaves. Like the Dark Mother, the soil is fertile here, a blend of new life where young tree saplings grow, stretching for the light, and old apple trees with twisted branches, exuding the energy of winter's old hag.

I find a dry spot to sit in the dark of the woods and lean up against the trunk of a tree, while tossing fallen apples to Libby. So much has changed since my trip to Egypt. The mysteries and the land felt so foreign to me when I first set foot on the dry, desert landscape. But now, I understand more each day the meaning of their hieroglyphs and their apparent devotion.

The ancient Egyptians honored the human body as the temple of the Divine and they celebrated the duality we experience here on earth. The sun and moon, the earth and sky, the bird and snake, man and woman. But their entire spiritual practice was to find oneness within duality. I am finally getting this. And my relationship with Ricardo and Hawk Circle continues to be such fertile ground for me to learn. Ricardo and I are opposite in so many ways, and in some cases, extreme opposites. Yet, in the tiniest of moments, I experience powerful transformation when I'm willing to let go of my stories about us, or about him. I realize separation and division is such an illusion, and I wonder if this is our sole task here on earth, to heal this division in all areas of our lives. The division that is based on fear that compels us to pull back from another, leads us to believe we're not whole or worthy, or that we're better than another, separates us from our power and our own soul. Fear is a master at this, however, love, is more than a worthy opponent.

Love is the healer. Love is the golden thread that weaves together the deepest ravines and unites what was once divided.

I think back to a moment with Ricardo — a powerful moment. We had a pattern that would undoubtedly turn our conversations on end as we stormed off in opposite directions. On one occasion, we were talking, and there it was, this pattern, creeping in.

I stepped back, and asked myself the questions, "Am I willing to let go of the story? Am I willing to let go of needing to be right? Can I admit that maybe I don't know what is real and what isn't?"

It was a death of my ego and ideas that I relentlessly held onto. A threshold moment that led me to a completely different experience. Letting go of my worn out pattern of defense was scary. It was an act of faith. I stood on foreign ground and couldn't find the words to speak. But I didn't need to. My willingness to drop my old, worn out rhetoric was enough to shift the energy from a place of harsh struggle to a gentle welcoming of the other. Our dynamic that had played out over years, diminished. We moved closer to one another and felt love in our hearts and an acceptance for each other's viewpoint. It's the in-between space where love resides.

I realize that this is the task at hand — to be present with every small moment where I encounter struggle or division. My ties to the old world fabric are nothing but stories and outdated beliefs.

Letting them go opens the way to weaving a new world. Like a seed holding so much potential for life, the future is yet to be determined. It's in the present and the tiniest of moments where the greatest power of transformation lives.

I continue to apply this exercise to all other areas of my life where previously, struggle ensues. It's actually a simple recipe. Where there is struggle, there is fear. But the ties to fear are formidable and not easy to break.

I stand in the middle of a battleground between my ego and my authentic self. My ego clings to the old stories and beliefs, because without them, she is nothing. She fights to stay alive, but the minute I allow love to enter, she instantly turns to dust and is carried off by the wind.

I can see this situation through the eyes of love and transmute my experience.

This is the voice of my authentic self. Over and over again, I surrender to the power of love, letting go of my ego and my attachments and my old stories. It's like watching a movie and deciding to change the channel from fear to love. The reality I believed was real begins to fade, as love enters.

Fear is the greatest divider. It keeps nations divided. Our own country, races of people, families — all separated by fear.

Another area of separation that I struggle with is that of mind and body. I was taught mind over matter and to override what my body is telling me. I smiled, when sad. Was nice, when angry. Worked, when sick. Had sex, when wanting to sleep. Stayed, when wanting to run.

This is how we find ourselves in relationships with narcissists. We override what our gut and our instincts tell us. We talk ourselves into believing something quite different. Almost every woman I've helped traverse this landscape to free herself, remembers the moment when she disregarded her initial feeling. Her mind convinced her that he was caring when her body was telling her the exact opposite.

Libby lays down next to me to rest, tired from chasing apples. A slight breeze blows, stirring up a few dried leaves, and they rise up, swirling in front of us. I recognize this type of occurrence as a visit from the Otherworld. I close my eyes and tune in. As I shift my awareness beyond the bounds of the physical world, I hear the voice of Mary Magdalene.

"See more of who you are," she says, in a deep, throaty voice.

As I ponder her words, my awareness goes to the Holy Isle of Iona. Some believe Iona to be the real Avalon and the place where the original grail lives deep underground. I recall the stories of the priestesses of the ank that resided there. The Druids that came later. Mother Mary, Joseph and Jesus' visit to the small, holy island to open a portal to the fountain of life. And later, Jesus and Mary Magdalene's visit to Iona, where together, they held a grail space for supernal consciousness to enter the earth for humanity. They were the true servers of the grail. They acted as the living bridge where the spiritual forces, represented by the sword, penetrated the grail of the earth, the Sacred Marriage.

My eyes open to the work I've been doing. While I walked the paths throughout the years, feeling blind, not seeing or understanding what I was doing, now the story is laid out before me. My heart's desire to create heaven on earth had been my internal compass all these years, based solely on pure faith. I think back to a passage I had read in Gareth Knight's book, *The Mystical Qabalah*. He speaks of the three tests of the initiate with faith being the most prominent.

I wonder how many there are of us, women, rooted in this ancient lineage, weaving heaven and earth together. We're spread out across the world with oceans between us, opening the gateways, becoming the grail so the supernal consciousness can seed our world. The Marys, the Maris, the Miari, the women from the sea.

My thoughts return to the small church in Limoux, France where Helena had pointed out the image of Mary Magdalene and her reversed hand position. She's been telling me all along that what I've been taught is the complete reversal of the truth. What we seek isn't found outside of ourselves, it's within. And our longing for heaven and our search for the Divine is found in nature, not in the clouds. And to return home to the stars, is by way of the earth. R.J. Stewart said it best in his book, *The Underworld Initiations*, "If we go deep enough into the UnderWorld, we emerge among the Stars."

I grow tired from stretching my awareness to the outer most fringes.

"C'mon Libby! Let's go home."

Libby races ahead, down the trail, through the woods. I stop for a moment to collect wild raspberries along the way. I look up at the hills. A small revelation comes to me. Hawk Circle is neither a wilderness skills school or a spiritual center. It's a beautiful blending of what it means to be human.

I can see smoke coming out of our chimney. *Ricardo must be up, making a fire on this chilly morning.* The sweet smell of pancakes and maple syrup waft through the air as I open the door. Ricardo stands at the stove with spatula in hand, and Javi sits at the table. They both turn and smile as Libby and I walk in leaving the chill of the morning air behind us.

Chapter 22
Goodbye
Dear Friend

My beautiful mother with golden hair and blue eyes like the sky birthed me into this world. But you dear Helena, with dark, auburn hair and eyes that match the fertile soil of Mother Earth birthed my soul and awakened my spirit, guiding me into the mysteries once again.

I lie in bed longer than usual, extracting a message from my dream. The maple tree, just outside our window is transforming before my eyes into a canopy of deep orange and red. A female cardinal sits on a branch, barely visible with its soft, muted colors, chirping loudly, no doubt calling to her mate. I wait to see the flash of vivid red as he flies in to perch by her side, but he's too late. She lost her patience and flew off looking for him.

My attention returns to my dream. I remember Helena saying something to me, but it's a slippery memory. I piece together what little I recall and am left only with an image of me standing in Helena's kitchen. Glancing at the clock, I get out of bed, knowing it's too early to call her. An uneasy feeling lingers, so I throw on some clothes and head outdoors with Libby for my morning walk, hoping to shake off the uneasiness.

We walk to the pasture to check on the sheep and give them some hay. With our farm apprentices now gone, the tending of the sheep is all on me. I don't mind. They are beautiful, Icelandic sheep that we brought to Hawk Circle just a few years prior to help keep our pastures open. They pull me outdoors early, every morning, including the days where temperatures are well below zero in the winter, or in spring when rain pours down. As long as I'm appropriately dressed for the weather, I love it. It's a great way to start my day. Undisturbed, freshly fallen snow, heavy morning mist or sparkling dew, magnifying a spider's web is a feast for the eyes, on display for only the early morning risers.

I hear the guttural sounds of the sheep baaaaing as they notice me from afar. Sounding like a small stampede, they race from the pasture to greet me as I toss a bale of hay over their fence. Gretel, a creamy white sheep that was born the year prior steps over the hay and nuzzles me, her breath warming my hand.

"You're ready to get sheared, aren't you?" I say as I run my fingers through her long, thick wool that hangs down well past her legs.

I stand for a moment, my hands now soft with lanolin, and watch the sheep happily chew on the fresh hay, seeing their breath, like small clouds of warm air escaping and meeting the cold. Their wool is lightly coated with frost and glistens as the sun shines through the morning mist.

My thoughts return to Helena, and I head back inside to call her. Her familiar quick hello on the other end of the phone, follows her usual "Treeeeesta" warms my heart. So many times, over the years, I called her, desperate for advice, and hearing her voice instantly brought comfort to my frazzled state. She was always there, willing to share her wisdom, bring clarity to my fears, and when necessary, give me a kick in the butt. Over the past several years,

our relationship changed, and my calls are now more about checking in on her, making sure she's well and has what she needs.

She no longer offers her sacred journeys. Egypt was the last
trip she led. I wish I had known at the time it would be our last, I
would have savored every moment, made time stand still and taken
in the joy ten times more. I would have taken note of how much I
enjoyed watching her enter a temple, her small, short frame jump-
ing up on a rock so everyone in the group could hear her while she
taught and shared her wisdom. Her owl-like eyes that effortlessly
see into other dimensions, her hearty laughter around the dinner
table after a long day, and her all-knowing smile and a wink, letting me know she sees what I'm doing with my inner work and
full-heartedly approves. I miss her, but at the same time, I'm stepping into this role myself with young apprentices who stay at our
place. I love working with the people who come to Hawk Circle,
but stepping out into the world as a teacher and healer, beyond our
property, is an unsettling thought.

After talking to Helena, I understand what my dream is about.
She's getting ready to move from her home to a place where she
won't have to worry about the demands of taking care of a house,
a barn and her large piece of property. She'll also be closer to her
daughter and grandchildren. Realizing that I might never see her
again since she's going to be much further away, I plan to visit her
the following week.

I throw my overnight bag into the passenger side of the car and
turn, bumping into Ricardo.

"Here, bring this to Helena for your dinner tonight," he says
handing me a small venison roast.

"Oh, she'll love this. Thank you," I say giving him a kiss goodbye.

"And here's your scarf. I thought you might want it," he says as he gently drapes it around my neck. He pulls me close, and I bury my face in his soft flannel shirt, and inhale the sweet smell of wood he's been chopping all morning.

"Thanks sweetie. I'll call you later to check in on Javi."

Driving along the bumpy and narrow mountain road, I think back to the first time I met Helena. I was so young and naive and had no idea as to the world I was entering. I can't imagine what my life would look like if I hadn't followed through on my search for Helena. Would I still be in my first marriage, wasting away, my dying soul having never met its purpose? Would I be bitter or numb, or would I be so domesticated, forgetting the wild part of myself ever existed? I imagine there would be a time years later when my soul would rise and the feral cat in me would scratch its way out, tear away at the binding harness freeing myself from a life lived in fear.

Now, years later, I drive along the tiny dirt roads, leading to Helena's home and I'm confident at each turn that I'm on the right path, both finding her house and in my life.

Realizing this might be my last trip up her mountain road, I take notice of the little town that lays below and the beautiful forest. I'll have no other reason to return to this small town, ever again. It's funny how life is. People and places become such a big part of our lives, and then change happens. The town where Helena lives is where Matthew had first gone to pre-school. I remember him reluctantly walking into the school with his stuffed beaver under his arm, and now, he's preparing to leave for college the following year. Nearby, is also the town where I had taken Jessi to her first dance class as a toddler where the two of us danced and sang together. All the sweet memories this area holds for me. And then of course, there's Helena. The woman who opened me up to who I am, guided me into a world, once so foreign and now, part of my everyday life.

As my mind wanders beyond the bounds of my physical existence, I see Helena and myself in another time and place. Sister priestesses, teacher/student, midwives to the soul, medieval magicians, lifetimes working together and now this time, having found each other once again. I have students, too, that have felt as familiar. I watch them walking down the road carrying a basket filled with vegetables from the garden or carefully harvesting an herb for making medicine. They drift in and out of my present-day reality into a foreign landscape where I see them as a temple priestess.

I pull into Helena's driveway and sit for a moment taking in the beauty of the area. She has a weathered old barn behind her house that she renovated many years ago where she used to have students stay when she taught classes.

Her impeccably kept gardens overflowing with herbs and flowers and meandering trails leading into the woods, now succumb to the relentless weeds. I gather up my basket of eggs, jar of homemade jam, frozen venison that Ricardo sent along, and her favorite healing oils, and head to the house. Another woodpile like ours, stacked near the door. Countless, empty pots stacked in corners, waiting for another summer.

When I enter Helena's house, I pause, wanting to remember every detail. Still the same Waverly blue and white toile curtains hang in her kitchen and the hand-crafted, Turkish rug lays beneath her table as it did the first time I walked into her magical home so many years ago. Her statues and crystals that at one time spawned trepidation, now instill comfort, beautiful memories and powerful initiations. Her French doors open the way to her deck where fading blooms overflow from multi-colored flowerpots.

We spend the evening sitting at her table, eating Ricardo's venison roast with curried vegetables, while drinking red wine and sharing countless stories.

"Helena, remember the time when we were in Turkey and the police barricaded us?" I say, chuckling at the memory.

"Oh yes, when we were visiting the temple of the Amazonian women?" she giggles.

"That was pretty intense. They thought we were smuggling drugs or weapons, remember?" I ask.

"Hahahaha! That's right. We spent some time at the police station. Oh good goddess, Treeeesta. We did have some fun, didn't we?" says Helena smiling from ear to ear.

I brought my camera with me and ask Helena if I can "interview" her and record her speaking so I can share it with my students. They've heard Helena's name mentioned so many times, and I want to make sure I have something of her to share with them. Helena seems to enjoy this idea and quickly takes a seat, straightening her back and taking on the posture of the wise sage.

Recording her is a gift. She speaks so eloquently on the subject of carrying pain. She talks about the power and the importance of forgiveness and how toxic it is to our bodies when we don't let go of our pain and our anger. She talks about earth's power points. But then, as she finishes sharing her wise words, she looks away from the camera and right at me. Her fierce eyes lock on mine. It's a moment that will be forever etched in my memory.

"You have to take people to these places," she says with conviction.

I shift my weight in my seat and turn my attention to the camera. She notices right away my attempt to brush this moment to the side. Leaning forward, she reaches out and touches my hand with the intent of holding my focus.

"No, not maybe, YOU have to take people to these places," she repeats.

It takes me a moment to digest that Helena is passing the torch onto me. Of all the people she's shared her work with and traveled with over a period of 30 plus years, she's passing the torch over to me. It's too much for me to take in all at once, and I squirm while muttering the word, "Yes." I'm speechless, my mind racing with how I'm going to pick up what she started. The thought is unnerving, having spent the past 20 years living at Hawk Circle, a safe distance from the world. *Am I ready to take this on? Can I guide the people as well as she did through the gates of initiation?* I fight the desire to flee from my destiny, as I tactfully change the subject. I accept what she's putting out as gracefully as possible, but I'm aware that I'm not ready to let go of the thought of her never offering another trip, or teaching. I have a hard time accepting that this moment we're sharing marks an end of an era.

Getting ready to leave the next day, to head back home, I give Helena what I think might just be my last hug goodbye and a kiss on the cheek. She feels smaller, more fragile, and I can tell she's lost weight as I carefully wrap my arms around her.

"Helena, you've given me so much in my life. Do you know how dear you are to me?" I say, my eyes filling with tears.

"Treeesta, as you are to me. It is your time now. Go, continue what we've started," says Helena with a quivering smile.

I get into my car and as I drive away, I turn and look back to see Helena wiping a tear from her eye. My heart aches with our memories of so many years spent together.

Driving down the mountain road one last time, I hear Helena's voice, softly whispering to me.

"We will meet in your dreams, dear Treeeesta, forever and for always." And this is exactly where we do meet again.

A few short years later, I head home from my morning walk, and I hear Helena's voice.

"I always wanted to visit your home," she says. "It's as beautiful as you described it."

I abruptly stop and stand perfectly still. My heart tells me what I don't want to hear.

"Helena, did you pass over?" I ask, my voice shaking.

I hear her familiar belly laugh.

Now, Helena continues to guide me from the other side.

This book is dedicated to Helena Shik.

A wise woman, an unknown mystic,

who quietly guided many people into the mysteries.

Made in the USA
Las Vegas, NV
28 November 2023

81713383R00144